The Heritage of British Literature

The Heritage of British Literature

With 114 illustrations, 14 in colour

ELIZABETH BOWEN
ANTHONY BURGESS
LORD DAVID CECIL
GRAHAM GREENE
KATE O'BRIEN

BOOK CLUB ASSOCIATES
LONDON

PUBLISHER'S NOTE

The essays by Elizabeth Bowen, Lord David Cecil, Graham Greene and Kate O'Brien were first published during the Second World War in the Britain in Pictures series, edited by W. J. Turner. A collected edition of seven volumes from the series, including those now republished, appeared in 1944 under the titles *Impressions of English Literature* (in the United Kingdom) and *The Romance of English Literature* (in the United States). For this newly illustrated edition, Lord David Cecil has added an epilogue to *The English Poets* and Anthony Burgess has written an Afterword discussing the developments of the postwar period.

This edition published 1983 by Book Club Associates
by arrangement with Thames and Hudson Ltd, London

Printed and bound in Great Britain

Contents

Poets

LORD DAVID CECIL

VERY great nation has expressed its spirit in art: generally in some particular form of art. The Italians are famous for their painting, the Germans for their music, the Russians for their novels. England is distinguished for her poets. A few of these, Shakespeare, Milton, Byron, are acknowledged to be among the supreme poets of the world. But there are many others besides these. Shakespeare is only the greatest among an array of names. Seven or eight other English poets deserve world-wide fame: in addition to them, many others in every age have written at least one poem that has made them immortal. The greatness of English poetry has been astonishingly continuous. German music and Italian painting flourished, at most, for two hundred years. England has gone on producing great poets from the fourteenth century to to-day: there is nothing like it in the history of the arts.

That the English should have chosen poetry as the chief channel for their artistic talent is the result partly of their circumstances, partly of their temperament.

English is a poet's language. It is ideally suited for description or for the expression of emotion. It is flexible, it is varied, it has an enormous vocabulary; able to convey every subtle diverse shade, to make vivid before the mental eye any picture it wishes to conjure up. Moreover its very richness helps it to evoke those indefinite moods, those visionary flights of fancy of which so much of the material of poetry is composed. There is no better language in the world for touching the heart and setting the imagination aflame.

English poetry has taken full advantage of its possibilities. Circumstances have helped it. Nature placed England in the Gothic North, the region of magic and shadows, of elves and ghosts, and romantic legend. But from an early period she has been in touch with classic civilization, with its culture, its sense of reality, its command of form. In consequence her poetry has got the best of two traditions. On the

Lord David Cecil, photographed in 1939.

The early fifteenth-century Ellesmere manuscript of The Canterbury Tales, *open at the beginning of the Wife of Bath's tale. The Wife herself – 'Boold was her face, and fair, and red of hewe . . .' – is shown on her horse. Her tale, a fairy story, is designed to show that women desire control over their husbands – she concludes: 'And eek I pray Jhesu shorte their lives | That will not be governed by their wives.'*

whole Nature has been a stronger influence than history. Most good English poets have been more Gothic than classical; inspired but unequal, memorable for their power to suggest atmosphere and their flashes of original beauty, rather than for their clear design, or their steady level of good writing. For the most part too, they write spontaneously, without reference to established rules of art. But they have often obeyed these rules, even when they were not conscious of them: and some, Milton and Chaucer for instance, are as exact in form and taste as any Frenchman. No generalization is uniformly true about English poetry. It spreads before us like a wild forest, a tangle of massive trees and luxuriantly-flowering branches, clamorous with bird song: but here and there art has cut a clearing in it and planted a delicate formal garden.

Roughly speaking, English poetry divides itself into four phases. The first, the medieval period, is a short one. During most of the Middle Ages neither language nor the laws of versification were sufficiently developed to be a vehicle for the best poetry. Only towards the middle of the fourteenth century were they ready. Even then, it is to be doubted if they would have revealed their possibilities without the genius of one man. Geoffrey Chaucer (1340?–1400) is the first great English poet; and he has remained one of the greatest. He was a story-teller. Of the two works for which he is remembered, the first, *Troilus and Criseyde*, re-tells a love romance about the siege of Troy; the second, *The Canterbury Tales*, is a collection of stories, serious and comic, supposed to be told by a troop of Pilgrims on their way to the Shrine of St Thomas of Canterbury. Chaucer is a curious mixture of the old and the new. In his subject matter he looks back to that world of medieval Christendom which was approaching its end. His stories were old stories; legendary romances and popular anecdotes. And he tells them in the straightforward spirit in which they were created. On the other hand his smooth easy style is something quite new; in his work we find the English language used for the first time to produce effects as delicate, artful and economical as those of the great writers of Greece and Rome. What is the life of man, he laments,

> Now with his love, now in the colde grave,
> Alone, withouten any company.

The sad fleetingness of mortal life, the solitude of death, is conveyed in thirteen words.

But Chaucer's mastery of style is only one of his gifts. He makes his stories enthralling, and his characters alive. The Canterbury Pilgrims, the fat, genial, gap-toothed wife of Bath, the gay young Squire, 'as fresh as is the month of May', the brutal miller with his red scaly neck, are as vivid as people we have met. And he can trace with the subtle sympathy of a psychological novelist the guilty waverings of poor frail Criseyde. Indeed, of all his talents, it is his sympathetic spirit that most compels our admiration. Here again his spirit shows a curious mixture of old and new. Chaucer approaches life with the innocent zest of an earlier civilization. He delights in spring flowers, in youthful beauty, in the animal humours of the body; a fresh gale, racy with the smell of earth, blows through his pages. But his attitude to life is not unsophisticated. He is a man of the world. He knows human nature well and has no illusions about it.

Acuteness and charity combine in an ironical wisdom which sparkles over his pages in a silvery sunlight.

Chaucer left no followers to compare with himself. During the fifteenth century, medieval civilization collapsed in a series of civil wars, and wars, as we know too well to-day, do not provide a favourable climate for poets. The only voices that made themselves heard above the storm were those of the anonymous, humble composers of popular ballads and carols. These, however, were enough to make the period memorable. The childlike sweetness of the carols, the wild lilt of the ballads, with their stark, tragic stories shrouded in an atmosphere of Gothic enchantment, disturbed the imagination and thrilled the heart with a direct sharpness, denied to most sophisticated poetry:

THE UNQUIET GRAVE

The wind doth blow to-day, my love,
And a few small drops of rain;
I never had but one true-love,
In cold grave she was lain.

I'll do as much for my true-love
As any young man may;
I'll sit and mourn all at her grave,
For a twelvemonth and a day.

The twelvemonth and a day being up,
The dead began to speak;
'Oh who sits weeping on my grave
And will not let me sleep?'

''Tis I, my love, sits on your grave,
And will not let you sleep;
For I crave one kiss of your clay-cold lips,
And that is all I seek.'

'You crave one kiss of my clay-cold lips;
But my breath smells earthy strong;
If you have one kiss of my clay-cold lips,
Your time will not be long.

"'Tis down in yonder garden green,
Love, where we used to walk,
The finest flower that ere was seen
Is withered to a stalk.

'The stalk is wither'd dry, my love,
So will our hearts decay;
So make yourself content, my love,
Till God calls you away.'

With the beginning of the sixteenth century, professional poetry began to raise its head again, led by the fantastic, playful Skelton and the graceful amorous verses, modelled on classic and Italian poetry, of Wyatt and Surrey. But it was not till the reign of Elizabeth that it emerged into full sunlight. The world that met its eyes was a changed world. England had broken with the Catholic Church, had established a new triumphant monarchy, and was on the way to lay the foundation of an Empire. Her new-born vitality and self-confidence expressed itself in a tremendous outburst of poetic talent. For a hundred years England was alive with poets, lyric poets, dramatic poets, narrative poets, philosophic poets; and among them the greatest she ever produced. Their work reflects the age they lived in, the Renaissance; a multi-coloured age, cruel, fantastic and glorious, mingling in a bewildering complexity, horror and beauty, barbarism and subtlety.

It passed through two phases. The first, the early Renaissance, was hopeful and joyous. After the darkness of the preceding age, man rioted in his newly discovered sense of life's splendour. This poetry is sumptuous and musical in form, in mood it is ideal and magnificent. The chief figure among non-dramatic poets is Edmund Spenser (1552?–99). His great work, *The Faerie Queene*, is a long symphonic poem, in the form of a fairy-tale romance about knights and ladies, composed in celebration of Queen Elizabeth, and in praise of those noble qualities to which it should be the aim of her subjects to aspire. Still medieval in its feeling for the magical and the marvellous, it blends the idealism of chivalry, its belief in piety and heroism and poetic love, with a pagan delight in sensuous beauty. It is a strange mixture. Venus and King Arthur, the arch-angel Gabriel and Queen Elizabeth, jostle one another in an endless confusion of fabulous adventure. But this confusion is more than made up for by Spenser's poetic intensity. An iridescent glow of beauty suffuses his whole canvas, harmonizing its most incongruous elements, and breathing forth

'The percing steele there wrought a wound full wyde, | That with the uncouth smart the Monster lowdly cryde.' The Red Cross Knight fights the dragon: a woodcut from Spenser's The Faerie Queene (1590). Spenser intended that his epic should be divided into twelve books each concerned with a 'morall vertue' embodied in a knight whose adventures form the plot. The Red Cross Knight, who represents Holiness, is the hero of Book 1.

its spirit in a stream of melody, honeyed, dreamy, and intricate; which lulls the critical mind to sleep, like a spell woven by one of the poem's own sorcerers.

> Open the temple gates unto my love,
> Open them wide that she may enter in,
> And all the posts adorn as doth behove,
> And all the pillars deck with garlands trim,
> For to receive this Saint with honour due,
> That cometh in to you.
> With trembling steps and humble reverence,
> She cometh in, before th'Almighty's view;
> Of her ye virgins learn obedience,
> When so ye come into those holy places,
> To humble your proud faces:
> Bring her up to th'high altar, that she may
> The sacred ceremonies there partake,
> The which do endless matrimony make;
> And let the roaring organs loudly play
> The praises of the Lord in lively notes;
> The whiles, with hollow throats,
> The choristers the joyous anthem sing,
> That all the woods may answer and their echo ring.
>
> *From 'Epithalamion'*

At the same time a school of courtly poets arose – Sir Walter Raleigh and Sir Philip Sidney are the most famous of them – who expressed a similar spirit on a smaller scale. In mellifluous and flowered phrase, they carol of silken dalliance and Arcadian shepherds, of winged Cupid and the rose of pleasure that must be plucked ere it withers. In a sense, these poems are artificial productions; sentiment and imagery alike are conventional; in another sense they are as natural as the song of birds; spontaneous outpourings of youthful fancy, intoxicated by the loveliness of the world.

> The fields breathe sweet, the daisies kiss our feet,
> Young lovers meet, old wives a-sunning sit,
> In every street these tunes our ears do greet—
> Cuckoo, jug-jug, pu-we, to-witta-woo!
> Spring, the sweet Spring!
>
> *From 'Spring' by Thomas Nashe*

Sir Walter Raleigh (c. 1552–1618) – courtier, adventurer and lyric poet: the quintessential Elizabethan gentleman. A miniature by Nicholas Hilliard of about 1585.

A similar intoxication permeates the other great literary form of the period, the drama. Otherwise it was very different, not courtly and formal, but haphazard, racy and popular. The Elizabethan theatre was, at its inception, a very humble affair, controlled by troops of vagabond mummers, who roamed about from inn to great house providing entertainment for any one they could attract to their performances. It was a crude sort of entertainment too; its lighter pieces were a mixture of coarse farce and naïve, fairy-tale plot, relieved by singing and dancing; while its more serious efforts were incoherent melodramas made lively by as many ghosts and massacres and maniacs as could be packed into them. Such a drama did not rise to the level of literature at all. Indeed it might never have done so, had it not been that a poor bohemian scholar, Marlowe (1564–93), turned to the theatre as a means of making a living. Considered purely as a playwright, Marlowe was not much improvement on his predecessors. He had no sense of character and no gift of construction. But he was a dramatic poet of genius: and, in his hands, these rough melodramas were transfigured into a vehicle for the soul-stirring expression of human passion.

Faustus: Ah Faustus,
Now hast thou but one bare hower to liue,
And then thou must be damnd perpetually:
Stand stil you euer moouing spheres of heauen,
That time may cease, and midnight neuer come;
Faire Natures eie, rise, rise againe, and make
Perpetuall day, or let this houre be but
A yeere, a moneth, a weeke, a naturall day,
That Faustus may repent, and saue his soule,
O lente, lente currite noctis equi:

Faustus summons Mephistopheles: *the title-page of the 1620 edition of Marlowe's* Dr Faustus. *In return for Faustus's soul Mephistopheles offers him twenty-four years of life and anything he desires.*

The starres mooue stil, time runs, the clocke wil strike,
The diuel wil come, and Faustus must be damnd.

Dr Faustus, lines 1419–30

In line after line of triumphant eloquence, Marlowe trumpets forth Elizabethan pride in man's strength and beauty, his insatiable thirst for every joy, sensual and intellectual, that life could offer.

He was followed by a writer who, to a poetic genius even richer than his own, added that talent for design and character drawing that he lacked. The peculiar significance of Shakespeare (1564–1616) in the history of English literature arises from the fact that it was he alone who had the capacity to impose order on the brilliant chaos of Elizabethan drama. He was not a revolutionary. His comedies and tragedies are compounded of the same elements as those of his contemporaries. They are the same extraordinary mixture of beauty and farce and improbable horrors. But the apparent defects of the form become in his hands virtues. The breadth and flexibility of his imagination enabled him to unite these elements into a whole, and to make use of their diversity to present a wider range of experience than could have been included in any stricter form.

Hamlet: To die, to sleep;
To sleep: perchance to dream: ay, there's the rub;
For in that sleep of death what dreams may come
When we have shuffled off this mortal coil,
Must give us pause: there's the respect
That makes calamity of so long life;
For who would bear the whips and scorns of time,
The oppressor's wrong, the proud man's contumely,
The pangs of despised love, the law's delay,
The insolence of office and the spurns
That patient merit of the unworthy takes,
When he himself might his quietus make,
With a bare bodkin? who would fardels bear,
To grunt and sweat under a weary life,
But that the dread of something after death,
The undiscover'd country from whose bourn
No traveller returns, puzzles the will
And makes us rather bear those ills we have
Than fly to others that we know not of?

From Hamlet, *Act III, Scene 1*

In his most characteristic plays, *Hamlet* and *Antony and Cleopatra*, he shows us life in its variety; he ranges from tragic passion to ironical comedy, from solid realistic portraiture to ethereal lyric beauty. Yet all is fused into a whole, by the life-giving form of his imagination. It does not matter if his stories are improbable: the people in them are so living that we believe anything that we are told of them. It does not matter that his plays are such a mixture: we only feel them truer to the heterogeneous nature of life. He has his limitations. Absorbed as he was in the huge spectacle of human existence moving before his gaze, his eye never wanders to explore the realms of spiritual light and darkness extending beyond the brief span of mortal experience.

> We are such stuff
> As dreams are made on, and our little life
> Is rounded with a sleep.

So runs the brief, baffled comment in which, in his last play, he seems to sum up his final conclusions on the riddle of human destiny. He is the supreme spectator; content to report what he sees, and to let us draw a lesson from it, if we can.

His specifically poetic quality is of a piece with the rest of his work. Shakespeare's is a dramatic style, designed to convey as realistically as possible the flux of thought and feeling passing through the minds of his characters. To achieve this object he uses every means; breaks the ordinary rules of grammar and syntax, coins words of his own and employs any sort of language, from slang to the most ornate poetic diction, without regard to conventional canons of style. He can write with classic restraint; but his genius is of the English and Gothic type, bold and fantastic, its simplest statement thickly embroidered with the images of his exuberant fancy. On occasion, his invention over-reaches itself. In his efforts to extend the frontiers of expression, he becomes obscure or bombastic; sometimes, too, his delight in his command over words leads him into playing tricks with them, inexcusable by any standard of good taste. But when all is said he has the most wonderful style in the world, able to convey at once a subtler and wider range of feeling than any other and in which word and thought are so closely identified that it is impossible to paraphrase his lines without losing their essential significance; while to crown all, he writes with a natural imperial magic that makes the work of other writers seem pale or laboured by comparison.

SONNET XXIX

> When, in disgrace with Fortune and men's eyes,
> I all alone beweep my outcast state,
> And trouble deaf heaven with my bootless cries,
> And look upon myself, and curse my fate,
> Wishing me like to one more rich in hope,
> Featured like him, like him with friends possest,
> Desiring this man's art and that man's scope,
> With that I most enjoy contented least;
> Yet in these thoughts myself almost despising—
> Haply I think on thee: and then my state,
> Like to the Lark at break of day arising,
> From sullen earth, sings hymns at Heaven's gate;
> For thy sweet love rememb'red such wealth brings
> That then I scorn to change my state with kings.

Shakespeare's early work is gorgeous and sunshiny; in maturity it is complex, sombre, weighed down with the burden of thought. Here his work is a bridge between the first Renaissance period and the second. For the golden confidence of Spenser and Marlowe did not last long. How should it? 'The glories of our blood and state are shadows, not substantial things.' And those who pursue them most recklessly, are the soonest to discover their vanity. The poets of the later Renaissance retained the vitality of the earlier: life to them remained equally fascinating. But they did not trust it in the same way. With anguish they recognized that its pleasures and achievements are transitory; they are incessantly aware of the inevitability of death, the mysterious uncertainty of fate, the appalling possibilities of sin and suffering inherent in the very nature of human existence. The dramas of the great playwrights who followed Shakespeare: Webster, Tourneur, Ford, are glittering nightmares in which figures of baleful splendour burn their lives out against a lurid background of blood and mania and supernatural darkness. Even the one great comedian of the period, Ben Jonson (1573–1637), is touched with the same spirit. With fierce laughter, he ruthlessly exposes the monstrous pageant of human vice and folly.

Non-dramatic poetry shows the same change of heart. It is dominated by one man, John Donne (1573–1631). Donne is the epitome of the new age. In youth a passionate amorist, in age a passionate mystic, he thirsted as unappeasably as Marlowe himself for the absolute and the perfect. But a

John Donne's monument in St Paul's Cathedral, where he was appointed Dean in 1621. According to tradition, Donne, who died in 1631, posed for it by standing on a wooden urn and wrapping his shroud about him – a characteristic gesture by a man whose religious poems face death with faith and wit. The effigy was carved by Nicholas Stone.

darker temperament, reinforced by the questionings of a restless powerful intelligence taught him that such perfection is never achieved in this world. Now and again he reaches his ideal; passion and intellect fuse together to attain a white heat of sensual or spiritual ecstasy unique in English poetry. More often, however, they struggle with one another in labyrinths of baffled thought. His mode of expression faithfully mirrors his divided spirit. Gone is the smooth sweetness of Spenser and his friends.

Donne's language is colloquial, his rhythms complex, his imagery audacious and grotesque. For pages together he speaks in harsh and puzzling riddles; then suddenly comes a passage whose every word quivers, shining and transparent as a living flame.

> Dear Love, for nothing less than thee
> Would I have broke this happy dream,
>   It was a theme
> For reason, much too strong for fantasy.
> Therefore thou waked'st me wisely; yet
> My dream thou brok'st not, but continued'st it.
> Thou art so true that thoughts of thee suffice
> To make dreams truths and fables histories;
> Enter these arms, for since thou thought'st it best
> Not to dream all my dream, let's act the rest.
>
> As lightning, or a taper's light,
> Thine eyes, and not thy noise, waked me;
>   Yet I thought thee—
> For thou lov'st truth—an angel, at first sight;
> But when I saw thou saw'st my heart,
> And knew'st my thoughts beyond an angel's art
> When thou knew'st what I dreamt, when thou knew'st when
> Excess of joy would wake me, and cam'st then,
> I must confess it could not choose but be
> Profane to think thee anything but thee.

From 'The Dream'

'Donne', said Ben Jonson, 'was the first poet in the world in some things.' Certainly his contemporaries thought so. His influence was overwhelming. He had made lyrical poetry modern, individual and intellectual: after him it was almost impossible to go on writing in the conventional mode of the previous age. A host of writers appeared, ranging from pious clergymen to flaunting cavaliers, who sought to emulate Donne's boldness of style and fantastic ingenuities of thought. None of them was of his calibre of genius. But he had managed to communicate to them something of his intensity. So that they all have occasional flashes equal to the work of the greatest poets. Among the religious poets is the tender Herbert, the mystical Vaughan, the fiery Crashaw. The most famous of the secular are King, Carew, Suckling and the gallant Lovelace. Andrew Marvell (1621–78) is the least unequal of Donne's followers.

> Had we but World enough, and Time,
> This coyness Lady were no crime.
> We would sit down, and think which way
> To walk, and pass our long Loves Day . . .
>
> But at my back I alwaies hear
> Times winged Chariot hurrying near:
> And yonder all before us lye
> Deserts of vast eternity.
> Thy Beauty shall no more be found;
> Nor, in thy marble Vault, shall sound
> My echoing Song: then Worms shall try
> That long preserv'd Virginity:
> And your quaint Honour turn to dust;
> And into ashes all my Lust.
>
> *From 'To his Coy Mistress'*

Only two important writers withstood Donne's spell, Herrick and Milton. Herrick (1591–1674) is the least solemn of English poets. His pagan spirit was cheerfully impervious to melancholy thought. Gaily he continued to sing of springtime revels and light love, of curds and cream and nosegays. But he enjoyed them so freshly, he wrote with such a fanciful felicity that, touched by his hand, these withered flowers of poetry bloom anew, with a dew and immortal sweetness.

UPON JULIA'S CLOTHES

> Whenas in silks my Julia goes,
> Then, then (me thinks) how sweetly flowes
> That liquefaction of her clothes.

John Milton, painted in about 1629, when, at the age of twenty-one, he took his BA at Cambridge and wrote his first masterpiece, 'On the Morning of Christ's Nativity'.

> Next, when I cast mine eyes and see
> That brave Vibration each way free;
> Oh how that glittering taketh me!

There is nothing trifling about Milton (1608–74). A scholar, a philosopher and a puritan, he thought all except the most elevated type of poetry not worth the writing, and from an early age he made it his object to be the great English master of such poetry, to enshrine in imperishable words the highest truths known to man. Such an ambition revealed an awe-inspiring confidence in his own powers. But it was justified. Milton's genius united, in a unique way, heroic loftiness of spirit with the most delicate sensibility to every kind of sensuous beauty. He was also, alike in design and detail, a master of his craft. His early work is jewelled and fanciful; the great religious poems of his later years are sublime and austere. But each is equally remarkable for the grandeur with which it is conceived and the lucid perfection with which it is executed.

DESCRIPTION OF SATAN AND THE FALLEN ANGELS

He above the rest
In shape and gesture proudly eminent
Stood like a Towr; his form had yet not lost
All her Original brightness, nor appear'd
Less than Arch Angel ruind, and th' excess
Of Glory obscur'd: As when the Sun new ris'n
Looks through the Horizontal misty Air
Shorn of his Beams, or from behind the Moon
In dim Eclipse disastrous twilight sheds
On half the Nations, and with fear of change
Perplexes Monarchs. Dark'n'd so, yet shon
Above them all th' Arch Angel: but his face
Deep scars of Thunder had intrencht, and care
Sat on his faded cheek, but under Browes
Of dauntless courage, and considerate Pride
Waiting revenge.

From Paradise Lost, *Book 1*

Milton is the great example in English literature of that un-English type, the conscious artist; whose every effect is carried out in accordance with the rules of a refined and disciplined taste. His style is all marble and precious stones; it lacks Shakespeare's flexibility and still more his natural magic; but it is incapable of Shakespeare's lapses.

AT A SOLEMN MUSICK

Blest pair of Sirens, pledges of Heav'ns joy,
Sphear-born harmonious sisters, Voice, and Vers,
Wed your divine sounds, and mixt power employ
Dead things with inbreath'd sense able to pierce,
And to our high-rais'd phantasie present,
That undisturbed Song of pure content,
Ay sung before the saphire-coloured throne
To him that sits thereon
With saintly shout, and solemn Jubily,
Where the bright Seraphim in burning row
Their loud up-lifted Angel trumpets blow,
And the Cherubick host in thousand quires,

Touch their immortal Harps of golden wires,
With those just Spirits that wear victorious Palms,
Hymns devout and holy Psalms
Singing everlastingly;
That we on Earth with undiscording voice
May rightly answer that melodious noise;
As once we did, till disproportion'd sin
Jarr'd against natures chime, and with harsh din
Broke the fair musick that all creatures made
To their great Lord, whose love their motion sway'd
In perfect Diapason, whilst they stood
In first obedience, and their state of good.
O may we soon again renew that Song,
And keep in tune with Heav'n till God ere long
To his celestial consort us unite,
To live with him, and sing in endless morn of light.

Milton marks the end of the great age. His life coincided with those civil and religious wars, in which the English Renaissance sank to extinction. The period which succeeded it was without the sensual and spiritual splendour of its predecessor; it lacked, also, its confusion and its extravagance. England in the late seventeenth and eighteenth centuries was a society settled in civilized equilibrium, untroubled by fundamental issues, and in which questions of conduct and manners were discussed by the standards of good sense and good taste. Such a society expressed itself in a very different sort of poetry from what had gone before; so different that subsequent generations, dazzled by the glories of the age of Shakespeare, have often denied that it was poetry at all.

This shows, however, a foolishly narrow conception of poetry. The poets of this third phase may not be of the highest kind; but they have expressed perfectly certain aspects of human experience, not treated by other English poets. Theirs is predominantly social poetry. It deals not with the elemental passions of man, nor with his solitary dreams and visions, but with those subjects that interest him as a member of an organized society with established standards and conventions. It is the poetry of home and town and fashionable life, of friendship, flirtation and worldly wisdom: it voices the normal person's affections and his reflections on the way of the world. Its most characteristic forms are satire, didactic verse and poems of graceful compliment. When it fails it is commonplace and conventional; it is successful by reason of its wit, elegance and rhetorical force.

Dryden (1631–1700), who introduced the new style of poetry, is the least personal of English poets. He was a great critic; and even in his creative work he seems stimulated to write less by desire to communicate an individual vision, than by his pleasure in practising the craft of letters. In consequence he is at his best in satire, where his wit and vigour of mind compensate for any lack of more imaginative qualities. But he tried his hand at many other forms, songs, plays, stories; and always with a fair degree of success. His most commonplace thoughts are warmed into poetry by the sheer virile accomplishment of his writing, the swing and snap of his superb versification.

ZIMRI

Some of their chiefs were princes of the land;
In the first rank of these did Zimri stand,
A man so various that he seemed to be
Not one, but all mankind's epitome;
Stiff in opinions, always in the wrong,
Was everything by starts and nothing long;
But in the course of one revolving moon
Was chymist, fiddler, statesman, and buffoon;
Then all for women, painting, rhyming, drinking,
Besides ten thousand freaks that died in thinking.
Blest madman, who could every hour employ,
With something new to wish or to enjoy!
Railing and praising were his usual themes,
And both, to show his judgment, in extremes:
So over violent or over civil
That every man with him was God or Devil.
In squandering wealth was his peculiar art;
Nothing went unrewarded but desert.
Beggared by fools whom still he found too late,
He had his jest, and they had his estate.

His most famous successor, Pope (1688–1744), is also a master of his craft; not so varied but with an extremely delicate sense of style which he polished to the last degree of gleaming finish. Like that of the spider in one of his own poems, Pope's touch: 'So exquisitely fine, feels in each thread and lives along the line.' As Dryden represents the strength of the new school, so Pope represents its elegance, its acute perception of detail in character and custom, and all intensified by the fire of his peculiar and waspish temperament. In his satires hate becomes positively beautiful, a glittering rapier piercing the heart of its victim with one graceful deadly thrust; his lighter poems, notably _The Rape of the Lock_, a fantasy about fashionable life, are the very triumph of artifice. The frills and airy frivolity of the beau monde are crystallized into sparkling immortality by the brilliance of his art.

THE LADY'S DRESSING TABLE

And now, unveil'd, the Toilet stands display'd,
Each silver Vase in mystic order laid.
This casket India's glowing gems unlocks,
And all Arabia breathes from yonder box.
The Tortoise here and Elephant unite,
Transform'd to combs, the speckled, and the white.
Here files of pins extend their shining rows,
Puffs, Powders, Patches, Bibles, Billet-doux.
Now awful Beauty puts on all its arms;
The fair each moment rises in her charms,
Repairs her smiles, awakens every grace,
And calls forth all the wonders of her face.

From The Rape of the Lock, _Canto 1_

Pope set the standard of taste for his age. Indeed for sixty years after his death, writers, some of them very gifted, like Goldsmith and Dr Johnson, took him as their model. He had, however, reached perfection in his kind; and none of his followers equalled him. Fortunately, some poets did not try. The eighteenth century saw the rise of a number of authors – Thomson and Gray, Collins and Cowper, are the most famous of them – who turned from the urban and social subjects which had engaged the pens of Pope and Dryden, to sing in quieter strains of the pleasures of retirement. They represent no violent break with the prevailing tradition. As much as Dryden and Pope, they were rational and civilized persons, accepting the standards of society in which they lived: as much as Dryden

The Baron steals Belinda's lock: a detail from Beardsley's drawing of 1896 for The Savoy, *one of nine illustrating* The Rape of the Lock. *It perfectly captures the artifice and apparent frivolity of Pope's mock-heroic epic.*

and Pope they spoke for the average intelligent man of their day. Only they spoke for him in his more contemplative and sentimental moods. They express his love for friends and home, his sober piety, his pleasure in the peaceful beauty of the countryside. As life becomes more urban, people grow more consciously appreciative of nature as such. Spenser and Milton do not draw any careful distinction between natural beauty and other beauty; they enjoy both because they are beautiful. To Thomson (1700–48) and Cowper (1731–1800), the untutored charm of the rural and the rustic makes a peculiar appeal; living in a sophisticated world, the unsophisticated has for them the attraction of contrast, and their eighteenth-century eye for reality makes them describe it with delightful accuracy. The English landscape appears in their pages just as it is, undisguised by the extravagance of poetic fancy. Thomson, with his grassy distances stretching beneath sun-lit or cloudy skies, paints the broader view of it: Cowper's is more delicately exact in detail. He is memorable too as the only distinguished poet who has found his chief inspiration in domesticity, in the Englishman's characteristic tenderness for the simple pleasures and steadfast affections of home life, his sentiment for his own house, his own garden, his own pet animals.

EPITAPH ON A TAME HARE

Here lies, whom hound did ne'er pursue,
  Nor swifter greyhound follow,
Whose foot ne'er tainted morning dew,
  Nor ear heard huntsman's halloo; . . .

Old Tiney, surliest of his kind,
  Who, nursed with tender care,
And to domestic hounds confined,
  Was still a wild Jack hare. . . .

His diet was of wheaten bread,
  And milk, and oats, and straw;
Thistles, or lettuces instead,
  With sand to scour his maw. . . .

But now beneath this walnut shade
  He finds his long last home,
And waits, in snug concealment laid,
  Till gentler Puss shall come.

Gray (1716–71) and Collins (1721–59) are less fertile writers. Their combined works only make up a slender volume of elegiac verses, in most of which pensive reflection is diversified by occasional vignettes of landscape. In Collins' poems these vignettes play the largest part; he was the more imaginative of the two. Gray had a greater mastery of design, strengthened by a deeper note of sentiment.

In neither do we find the warmth of temperament necessary to raise them to the highest levels of poetry. But both have achieved a permanent place in English letters, by the purity of their inspiration, and the scholarly grace with which they have clothed it.

(right) *'Romney has drawn me in crayons, and in the opinion of all here with his best hand, and with the most exact resemblance possible'* wrote Cowper of this portrait of 1792.

(below) *This frontispiece of 1769 to Gray's 'Elegy Written in a Country Churchyard' embodies the contemplative poignancy of a poem which helped create a European vogue for verses of graveyard meditations.*

Some village-Hampden, that with dauntless breast
    The little Tyrant of his fields withstood,
Some mute inglorious Milton here may rest,
    Some Cromwell guiltless of his country's blood.

Th' applause of list'ning senates to command,
    The threats of pain and ruin to despise,
To scatter plenty o'er a smiling land,
    And read their hist'ry in a nation's eyes,

Their lot forbad: nor circumscrib'd alone
    Their growing virtues, but their crimes confin'd;
Forbad to wade through slaughter to a throne,
    And shut the gates of mercy on mankind, . . .

Far from the madding crowd's ignoble strife,
    Their sober wishes never learn'd to stray;
Along the cool sequester'd vale of life
    They kept the noiseless tenor of their way.
        From 'Elegy Written in a Country Churchyard' by Thomas Gray

How sleep the brave, who sink to rest,
By all their country's wishes blest!
When Spring, with dewy fingers cold,
Returns to deck their hallow'd mould,
She there shall dress a sweeter sod,
Than Fancy's feet have ever trod.
By fairy hands their knell is rung,
By forms unseen their dirge is sung;
Their Honour comes, a pilgrim gray,
To bless the turf that wraps their clay,
And Freedom shall awhile repair,
To dwell a weeping hermit there!
        From 'Ode Written in the Year 1746' by William Collins

   Both the urban and the country schools have left their mark on the
work of the last important writer in the eighteenth-century tradition.
George Crabbe (1754–1832) was not a polished artist. The long bleak
narratives of rural life which make up the greater part of his work are
often written in a style as bare as a guide-book; but there is something

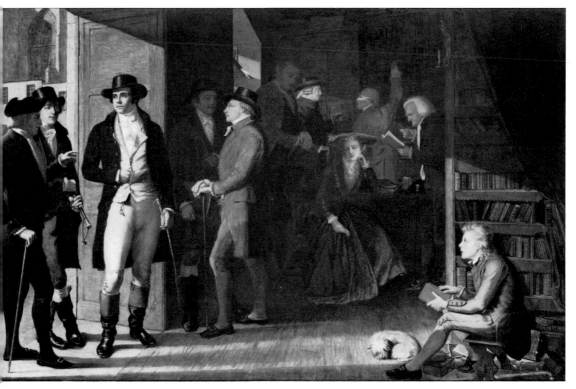

Sibbalds Circulating Library: *a nineteenth-century painting by the Scottish artist W. B. Johnstone, representing the literary society of Edinburgh in 1786 when the city – 'The Athens of the North' – was at the height of its intellectual reputation. Robert Burns stands in the doorway; behind him are (left) the sermon-writer Hugh Blair and (right) Henry Mackenzie, the essayist and novelist. Sitting on the right is the fifteen-year-old Walter Scott.*

compelling about them. The patient accuracy with which he observes the world, the unillusioned wisdom with which he judges it, make one listen to his words and forbid one to forget them.

From the general tradition of this period of English verse, two names stand apart. Robert Burns (1759–96), a Scottish peasant, founded his work on the popular songs of his own Lowland countryside, and it has the direct infectious zest and songfulness of a ballad. But heaven had made him a great artist; he added to the natural qualities of folk-poetry a grace, a finish and a humour of his own. The elemental feelings of humanity, the massive fun and pathos and passion of the natural man become, in his hands, the stuff of immortal poetry:

> Ye flowery banks o' bonnie Doon,
> How can ye blume sae fair!

How can ye chant ye little birds,
    And I sae fu' o' care!

Thou'll break my heart, thou bonnie bird,
    That sings upon the bough:
Thou minds me of the happy days,
    When my fause luve was true.

From 'The Banks o' Doon'

William Blake (1757–1827) is a more unusual type. He is in every respect a sensational contrast to his contemporaries. Possibly insane, and certainly inspired, he passed most of his time in a realm of mystical visions from which the material world was hardly visible, but which was astir with mysterious figures of demon and angel. An experience so remote from that of ordinary people makes much of Blake's work strange, and even unintelligible. But he had a lyrical gift of such unearthly power as to render this of almost no consequence. His fleeting fragments of song, his wild prophetic rhapsodies contain the distilled essence of poetry. They set the reader's nerves a-thrill with the inexplicable force of some natural manifestation, the cry of the birds, or the rush of the wind in the tree-tops.

Never seek to tell thy love,
    Love that never told can be;
For the gentle wind doth move
    Silently, invisibly.

I told my love, I told my love,
    I told her all my heart,
Trembling, cold, in ghastly fears,
    Ah! she did depart!

Soon after she was gone from me,
    A traveller came by,
Silently, invisibly:
    He took her with a sigh.

Canterbury Cathedral. '. . . from every shires end | Of Engelond to Caunterbury they wende | The hooly blisful martir for to seke. . .'. So Chaucer introduces The Canterbury Tales, *a collection of stories told by pilgrims journeying from London to the shrine of St Thomas à Becket in the cathedral. Chaucer includes himself among the pilgrims in his poem; it is thought that he made the journey in 1387.*

For centuries writers relied on the patronage of the nobility for their livelihoods. The Sackvilles, who owned Knole in Kent (left), had a great tradition of such sponsoring of literature. Thomas Sackville, the 1st Earl of Dorset, was the part-author of Gorboduc (1565), the first drama in blank verse (the poetic form brought to perfection by Shakespeare). The 3rd Earl entertained Jonson, Fletcher and Drayton here; Donne annually preached in the chapel. At the end of the seventeenth century the 6th Earl befriended Dryden and Prior. Knole is also the setting for Virginia Woolf's fantastical novel Orlando (1928), inspired by her relationship with Vita Sackville-West, born here in 1892.

(above) The interior of Milton's cottage at Chalfont St Giles, Buckinghamshire, to which the poet fled with his family in 1665 to escape the Great Plague. Here he completed Paradise Lost before returning to London in the following year.

(above) *Olney in Buckinghamshire, where the poet Cowper lived between 1767 and 1786. He taught at the Sunday school, wrote his* Olney Hymns *and helped his friend the evangelical curate, John Newton, who cared for him during the poet's recurrent depressions. After his recovery from one attack, the villagers gave him a young hare called Puss, the first of three owned by Cowper. The death of the second, Tiney, inspired the 'Epitaph on a Tame Hare'.*

Lord Burlington's villa at Chiswick in London (right) *is the creation of the greatest patron of literature and the arts in early eighteenth-century England. The villa became a meeting place for poets, architects and musicians, including Pope and Handel. The fourth of Pope's* Moral Essays, *'Of the Use of Riches', is addressed to Lord Burlington and admiringly discusses his attempts to introduce Palladian architecture and the art of landscape gardening into England, both represented to perfection at Chiswick.*

Romantic poets and novelists at the end of the
eighteenth century created a new, intense
appreciation of nature. Wordsworth's poetry,
embodying an almost mystical relationship
with the landscape of his native Lake
District, attracted numerous visitors to the
area eager to share his experiences. Among
them was De Quincey, whose white-washed
Nab Farm, visible in this view of Rydal
Water (above), was not far from
Wordsworth's home at Rydal Mount. De
Quincey's marriage to a social inferior excited
the strong disapproval of Wordsworth and his
sister and the friendship was ended. The
poems and novels of Walter Scott, which
reveal a deep feeling for the landscape around
his Border home, created a European vogue
for all things Scottish. This view of the
Eildon Hills (right) was a favourite of
Scott's; it was one of the last sights to rouse
him from semi-consciousness on his journey
home in his final illness.

Infant Joy

I have no name,
I am but two days old,—
What shall I call thee?
I happy am
Joy is my name,—
Sweet joy befall thee!

Pretty joy!
Sweet joy but two days old,
Sweet joy I call thee:
Thou dost smile,
I sing the while,
Sweet joy befall thee.

(above) *'Infant Joy', from William Blake's* Songs of Innocence *(1789); the poet etched the text and illustrations for the book, printed them and coloured them himself.*

Tennyson was born in Somersby, Lincolnshire, in 1809; the flat, marshy landscapes near his boyhood home provide the setting for many of his early poems: '. . . far through the marish green and still | The tangled water courses slept, | Shot over with purple, and green, and yellow.' ('The Dying Swan'.) This is a view of Gibraltar Point, by the mouth of the Steeping River, near which the poet loved to walk.

Blake lived before his time. His own age could not be expected to appreciate him; but in the forty years that followed his death, once more a revolution took place in English letters. Under the double shock of the Industrial and French Revolutions, the fabric of eighteenth-century civilization crumbled; its standard of taste and conduct lost their hold, and people turned for guidance to the instinctive movements of the heart and imagination. In politics and practical life this led to a good deal of confusion. Poetry however profited by the change. For passion and imagination are essential ingredients of the best poetry. Now, after a hundred years' repression, they flared up in the brightest blaze of poetic splendour since the Renaissance. It was marked by many of the same qualities. Glamour and mystery, extravagance and irregularity, fantasy and naïvety came thronging back into literature. But the poets of this new Romantic school, as it was called, were more consciously individualistic than the Elizabethans; reacting violently against the conventions that had governed their fathers, they deliberately followed the light of their vision wherever it might lead them. And they concentrated more on the inner life. They turned from the humdrum world to seek inspiration in the secret dreams of the fancy and the adventures of the solitary soul.

Wordsworth (1770–1850), the first great poet of the period, was a mystic of nature. The mountains of that Lake country of north-west England which was his home, its still waters and wooded silences communicated to him the sense of an indwelling spirit of the Universe, divine and beneficent, who would, if man listened to its voice, illuminate him with its own ineffable wisdom. To intepret this voice to mankind was the aim of all Wordsworth's poetry; and he thought this was best done by expressing himself in the plainest language, undisguised by the artificial ornaments of conscious art. Only a writer with the most impeccable natural taste could follow this principle without danger. Wordsworth was far from being such an author. The result is that his work is ludicrously unequal. Often it is as flat as the flattest prose. But now and then inspiration seizes him: and he rises to a height of serene, spiritual sublimity unparalleled in English poetry. Moreover, unlike Blake, he is never so wrapt into the world of his vision as to lose sight of the common earth. He is the supreme poet of spiritual experience, who can both convey those moments of celestial glory, in which man penetrates beyond the veil of the flesh, and also show them in their true relation to the confined prosaic round of every-day existence.

A daguerrotype of Wordsworth aged about seventy-seven. Poetic inspiration faded in his later life and he devoted much time to revising The Prelude, *his long autobiographical poem.*

But now, like one who rows,
Proud of his skill, to reach a chosen point
With an unswerving line, I fixed my view
Upon the summit of a craggy ridge,
The horizon's utmost boundary; far above
Was nothing but the stars and the grey sky.
She was an elfin pinnace; lustily
I dipped my oars into the silent lake,
And, as I rose upon the stroke, my boat
Went heaving through the water like a swan;
When, from behind that craggy steep till then
The horizon's bound, a huge peak, black and huge,
As if with voluntary power instinct
Upreared its head. I struck and struck again,
And growing still in stature the grim shape
Towered up between me and the stars, and still,
For so it seemed, with purpose of its own
And measured motion like a living thing,
Strode after me. With trembling oars I turned,
And through the silent water stole my way
Back to the covert of the willow tree;
There in her mooring-place I left my bark,—
And through the meadows homeward went, in grave
And serious mood; but after I had seen
That spectacle, for many days, my brain
Worked with a dim and undetermined sense
Of unknown modes of being; o'er my thoughts
There hung a darkness, call it solitude
Or blank desertion. No familiar shapes
Remained, no pleasant images of trees,
Of sea or sky, no colours of green fields;
But huge and mighty forms, that do not live
Like living men, moved slowly through the mind
By day, and were a trouble to my dreams.

From The Prelude, _Book 1_

Wordsworth's friend, Coleridge (1772–1834), had no such definite gospel to expound. He was a man of the most varied gifts, critic and philosopher as well as poet. And in each capacity, he exhibited gleams of extraordinary genius. But, owing to some inexplicable inability to concentrate his powers, they only found complete fulfilment in a handful of poems. The most famous of these, 'The Ancient Mariner', and 'Christabel', reveal another aspect of the romantic impulse, its sensibility to the imaginative appeal of the remote and the marvellous. In a succession of pictures, preternaturally vivid as those of a dream, and set to a haunting word music, they evoke the eerie enchantment of medieval legend.

> The moving Moon went up the sky,
> And nowhere did abide;
> Softly she was going up,
> And a star or two beside—
> Her beams bemock'd the sultry main,
> Like April hoar-frost spread;
> But where the ship's huge shadow lay,
> The charmed water burnt alway
> A still and awful red.
>
> Beyond the shadow of the ship,
> I watched the water-snakes:
> They moved in tracks of shining white,
> And when they rear'd, the elfish light
> Fell off in hoary flakes.
>
> Within the shadow of the ship,
> I watch'd their rich attire:
> Blue, glossy green, and velvet black,
> They coil'd and swam, and every track
> Was a flash of golden fire.
>
> *From 'The Ancient Mariner'*

A similar sensibility, but this time to the picturesque appeal of true history, is the outstanding characteristic of Sir Walter Scott's poems. Scott (1771–1832) was primarily a novelist; his rousing ballad tales in verse are poetry for boys rather than men. As such, however, they are as good as possible, stirring and gallant as the sight of a regiment stepping out to the sound of drum and bugle. The other romantic poets, Keats, Shelley, Byron, rise higher. Keats (1795–1821) like Coleridge responded to the attraction of medieval literature. But in him this was only one expression of a feeling for beauty of every kind. 'I have loved the principle of beauty in all things', he said, and the object of his poetry was to express this love.

On the first looking into Chapman's Homer

Much have I travell'd in the Realms of Gold,
   And many goodly States, and Kingdoms seen;
   Round many Western islands have I been,
Which Bards in fealty to Apollo hold.
Of one wide expanse had I been told,
   Which deep brow'd Homer ruled as his Demesne:
      Yet could I never judge what Men could mean,
Till I heard Chapman speak out loud and bold.
Then felt I like some Watcher of the Skies
   When a new Planet swims into his Ken,
Or like stout Cortez, when with wond'ring eyes
   He star'd at the Pacific, and all his Men
Look'd at each other with a wild surmise—
   Silent upon a Peak in Darien—

He was equipped to do it. Not only could he appreciate beauty in its most varied manifestations, but he had an extraordinary faculty for detecting precisely the qualities in which each specific manifestation consisted. Keats died very young, at the age of twenty-five, before he had learnt to discipline his exuberant talent; and some of his work is marred by a youthful floridity. But he had a gift for the right word, for the exact visualizing phrase, that can only be compared to Shakespeare's.

ON FIRST LOOKING INTO CHAPMAN'S HOMER

Much have I travell'd in the realms of gold,
    And many goodly states and kingdoms seen;
    Round many western islands have I been
Which bards in fealty to Apollo hold.
Oft of one wide expanse had I been told
    That deep-brow'd Homer ruled as his demesne;
    Yet did I never breathe its pure serene
Till I heard Chapman speak out loud and bold:
Then felt I like some watcher of the skies
    When a new planet swims into his ken;
Or like stout Cortez when with eagle eyes
    He stared at the Pacific—and all his men
Look'd at each other with a wild surmise—
    Silent, upon a peak in Darien.

In his pages, spring and autumn, the sensuous grace of classic myth, the moon-lit forests of fairy-tale, rise before the mental eye in all the detailed, breathing loveliness of reality.

Shelley (1792–1822) is the lyrical poet of the movement. Take it all in all, he is the most wonderful lyrical poet England has ever produced. In flight after flight of soaring, full-throated song he gives voice to those aspirations after an ideal freedom alike in love and politics, which surged in the breasts of the youth of his time. Youthfulness is one of Shelley's outstanding qualities. He has all youth's enthusiasm, its dreamy exaltation,

(below) *John Keats, sketched by his old school friend Charles Brown in 1819 at Shanklin.*
(above) *The autograph manuscript of Keats's first major poem, 'On First Looking into Chapman's Homer', written early one morning after a night spent excitedly reading Chapman with a friend. Keats has marked the rhyme scheme on the right; he altered the title and lines 6, 7 and 11 before publication in 1817.*

Shelley in the Baths of Caracalla, Rome, in 1819: a detail from a painting by Amelia Curran. He delighted in the spectacular, flower-strewn ruins amid which he continued work on his verse drama Prometheus Unbound.

its refusal to compromise with evil. Indeed, his idealism often made him very unhappy. His mood hovered between rapture at life as he wished it to be and despair at life as he found it. This division of spirit was, however, to the advantage of his poetry. For it kept it from becoming inhuman. His songs glow with an ethereal radiance, but they also throb with the poignancy of a soul who has known what it is to suffer.

> One word is too often profaned
>   For me to profane it;
> One feeling too falsely disdain'd
>   For thee to disdain it;
> One hope is too like despair
>   For prudence to smother;
> And pity from thee more dear
>   Than that from another.

> I can give not what men call love:
>   But wilt thou accept not
> The worship the heart lifts above
>   And the heavens reject not,
> The desire of the moth for the star,
>   Of the night for the morrow,
> The devotion to something afar
>   From the sphere of our sorrow?

There is nothing of Shelley's innocence about Byron (1788–1824). A dynamic, theatrical personality, ruthlessly observant of other people and morbidly sensitive to their opinion of himself he both lived and wrote with one eye fixed upon his audience. They returned his gaze. The figure of the beautiful Lord Byron with his reckless brilliance, and his shocking thrilling career of love and lawlessness, caught the imagination of the public as no poet ever has before or since. Since then a reaction has set in. Byron, in his own day far more admired than Keats or Shelley, is now rated below them. This is partly just; there is something coarse and stagey about his talent. But the decline of his reputation is also due to a passing fashion in taste. During the nineteenth century the standard of poetry was set by the other romantics; writers were admired in so far as they exhibited their sort of merit. Although Byron's life was romantic, his literary gifts were nearer those of Dryden and Pope. Like them he was a brilliant and eloquent commentator on the active life of man. And he was their equal. His best works, *Don Juan* and *The Vision of Judgment*, are written with a careless scintillating mastery that keeps them as vital now as the day they were written.

> My days of love are over; me no more
>   The charms of maid, wife, and still less of widow,
> Can make the fool of which they made before,—
>   In short, I must not lead the life I did do;
> The credulous hope of mutual minds is o'er,
>   The copious use of claret is forbid too,
> So for a good old-gentlemanly vice,
> I think I must take up with avarice.
>
> Ambition was my idol, which was broken
>   Before the shrines of Sorrow, and of Pleasure;

And the two last have left me many a token,
   O'er which reflection may be made at leisure:
Now, like Friar Bacon's brazen head, I've spoken,
   'Time is, Time was, Time's past;'—a chymic treasure
Is glittering youth, which I have spent betimes—
My heart in passion, and my head on rhymes.

From Don Juan, *Canto the First*

One other poet of this period must not be forgotten. Walter Savage Landor (1775–1864) is one of those authors who seem to have been created by Providence to show that there is an exception to every rule. He is equally far from the school of Pope and the school of the Romantics. The chief influence we can trace in his work is that of the ancient Latin writers. The epigrams which are his chief claim to fame, so grand in conception and so tersely expressed, are like antique inscriptions carved in marble to last for ever.

SEPARATION

There is a mountain and a wood between us,
    Where the lone shepherd and late bird have seen us
Morning and noon and eventide repass.
Between us now the mountain and the wood
Seem standing darker than last year they stood,
    And say we must not cross—alas! alas!

Meanwhile the tide of romanticism swept irresistibly on. Its first dazzling outburst came to an end with Byron. But the movement did not spend itself for a century and more; and produced a succession of poets who, if they never rose as high as their masters, maintained nevertheless a very high level. The first phase was distinguished by three figures, Tennyson, Browning and Matthew Arnold. Tennyson (1809–92) was, poetically speaking, the child of Keats; stimulated to write by a similar sensibility to beauty and with a natural gift for the lovely evocative phrase. He was a more accomplished craftsman, and his best work is a miracle of finished art. Only–he lacked Keats' divine fire. Perfectly though he expresses it, his vision of beauty has not the same inspired intensity; after Keats the best of Tennyson seems a little undistinguished. This lack of distinction was increased by the fact that he seldom allowed himself to concentrate exclusively on his vision. By the time he reached his maturity the Victorian age had begun to dawn over England. The Victorian age, strenuous and puritanical, took the view that poetry should teach a moral lesson. Tennyson yielded to the pressure of his age: he set up to be preacher as well as poet. And since his preaching did not spring from his native creative impulse, it was uninspired; a mere polished repetition of opinions held by serious persons of his day. All the same Tennyson is a great poet. No one since has left a volume of verse covering so wide a range of subject, with such consistent mastery of the art of writing. Moreover he has a special interest as one of the best painters of the English scene. Eastern and southern England are portrayed in his verses with the detailed accuracy of Cowper and a silvery exquisiteness of phrase, all his own.

Now fades the last long streak of snow,
    Now burgeons every maze of quick
    About the flowering square, and thick
By ashen roots the violets blow.

*Alfred, Lord Tennyson, in 1888; the book on his knee is a translation of the Odyssey –
which provided the inspiration for 'Ulysses', one of his finest poems.*

Now rings the woodland loud and long,
   The distance takes a lovelier hue,
   And drown'd in yonder living blue
The lark becomes a sightless song.

Now dance the lights on lawn and lea,
   The flocks are whiter down the vale,
   And milkier every milky sail
On winding stream or distant sea.

              From In Memoriam, *Canto CXV*

No one ever accused Browning (1812–89) of yielding to convention. In him, we find the wilful determination of the romantic to be himself at all costs, carried to its limit. The sort of poem he wrote – it was usually some spasmodic lyric or a dramatic monologue, put into the mouth of some curious imaginary character – is his own invention; so is his philosophy, a defiant optimism, boisterously welcoming disaster as a test of its strength. Most individual of all is his actual style; conversational, slap-dash, and freaked all over with the grotesque quips of Browning's fancy. So aggressively eccentric an author will never please every one. And it must be admitted Browning is often obscure and ugly. But he is most exciting reading: bursting with life and passion and possessed of a subtle insight into the processes of men's minds. He is also a most important influence, for what is looked on as the very 'modern' type of poetry, the complex, realistic, intellectual poetry of Mr T. S. Eliot and his followers, derives directly from Browning.

LOVE IN A LIFE

Room after room,
I hunt the house through
We inhabit together.
Heart, fear nothing, for, heart, thou shalt find her,
Next time, herself!—not the trouble behind her

Left in the curtain, the couch's perfume!
As she brush'd it, the cornice-wreath blossom'd anew
Yon looking-glass gleam'd at the wave of her feather.

Yet the day wears,
And door succeeds door;

I try the fresh fortune—
Range the wide house from the wing to the centre.
Still the same chance! she goes out as I enter.
Spend my whole day in the quest,—who cares?
But 'tis twilight you see,—with such suites to explore,
Such closets to search, such alcoves to importune!

Matthew Arnold (1822–88) was a less original writer. He was a serious-minded academic person, learned in the literature of the past; his style is a careful blending of Wordsworth and the classics. In consequence it never stirs us with the first-hand creative freshness of Browning or Tennyson. But this deficiency is partly counterbalanced by a greater depth of sentiment. In words of restrained and poignant eloquence, Arnold voices the profound melancholy which was beginning to permeate the more thoughtful minds of his time. For, in spite of its outward prosperity, and the extraordinary advance of material improvement which it witnessed, the Victorian age was not serene. Intellectually it was disordered; the revolutionary movement, which preceded it, had failed to establish any foundation of commonly accepted ideals, on which confidence in life might securely rest itself; religious faith was shaken by the discoveries of science. Darkly, the huge energy of material progress swept onwards to no certain end. This uncertainty affected the writers of the age and it was rendered still more painful for them by the fact that the new industrial civilization, which was bit by bit superseding the old England, tended to look on literature as a frivolous luxury, unrelated to the serious business of life. In consequence, the poets themselves grew more and more to feel at odds with the world in which they lived. Some turned their backs on it to take shelter in some secluded monastery of the imagination, constructed by themselves: others, embracing the philosophy of pessimism, openly repudiated life as a cheat. They can hardly be blamed. But it was a pity. It is not healthy for the artist to feel himself out of tune with the people round him. He becomes cranky or narrow or both. Whether for this cause or not, the poets of the later nineteenth century seem built on a smaller scale than their predecessors.

However they remained very good in quality. And there were a great many of them. The Pre-Raphaelite group, led by Rossetti (1828–82) and William Morris (1834–96) in his earliest, most fruitful phase, found refuge in an artistic dreamland founded on the art and literature of the Middle Ages and early Renaissance. It was an artificial place. And their poetry is a

Matthew Arnold in 1883, with his dachshund Max. The death of Max's predecessor, Geist, was recorded by Arnold in a poem, 'Geist's Grave'.

little artificial: languid, over-decorated, and self-conscious. But it does achieve the beauty which is its object. Morris's clear-coloured medieval landscapes, with their belfried towns peopled by troops of heraldic figures, Rossetti's sultry Italian splendours, made melancholy by a brooding autumnal passion – these can still delight the eye of the imagination.

NEAR AVALON

A ship with shield before the sun,
Six maidens round the mast,
A red-gold crown on every one,
A green gown on the last.

The fluttering green banners there
Are wrought with ladies' heads most fair,
And a portraiture of Guenevere
The middle of each sail doth bear.

A ship with sails before the wind,
And round the helm six knights,
Their heaumes are on, whereby, half blind,
They pass by many sights.

William Morris

Associated with these poets was Swinburne. Unlike theirs, his was a lyrical talent, deriving from Shelley rather than Keats: and though he too was deliberately archaic in style, he was not so exclusively Pre-Raphaelite. His dream world included elements taken from the Greeks and the Bible. Books rather than life were his inspiration. Indeed he had so little of his own to say, that his poetry is at times almost meaningless. But it too had beauty; surging forth in a torrent of orchestral music, all a-shimmer with sumptuous words.

Swinburne, in so far as he had a philosophy, was a pessimist, tumultuously lamenting the vanity of all things human. Here he links on to the declared pessimists. In Edward FitzGerald's *Rubáiyát of Omar Khayyám*, a very free adaptation from the Persian, pessimism was combined with a keen sensibility to pleasure. FitzGerald is a most original writer, mingling an eighteenth-century wit and precision, with a dreamy Oriental exoticism of mood. Since all ends in dust, is the burden of his song, let us enjoy ourselves while we can. Nowhere else in English is this ancient philosophy expressed so memorably as in his chiming, tolling stanzas.

Ah, my Beloved, fill the Cup that clears
Today of past Regrets and future Fears—
    Tomorrow?—Why, Tomorrow I may be
Myself with Yesterday's Sev'n Thousand years.

Lo! some we loved, the loveliest and best
That Time and Fate of all their Vintage prest,
    Have drunk their Cup a Round or two before,
And one by one crept silently to Rest.

And we, that now make merry in the Room
They left, and Summer dresses in new Bloom,
   Ourselves must we beneath the Couch of Earth
Descend, ourselves to make a Couch—for whom?

Ah, make the most of what we yet may spend,
Before we too into the Dust descend;
   Dust into Dust, and under Dust, to lie,
Sans Wine, sans Song, sans Singer, and—sans End!...
                    From The Rubáiyát of Omar Khayyám

Equally beautiful, equally without hope, are the lyrics of A. E. Housman, a Cambridge scholar, who came to maturity at the end of the century. Here the setting is not Oriental but rural. He called himself the Shropshire lad; and his pages are full of exquisite brief glimpses of the English landscape. But these only form an ironical background to a pessimism more intense than FitzGerald's.

Into my heart an air that kills
   From yon far country blows:
What are those blue remembered hills,
   What spires, what farms are those?

That is the land of lost content,
   I see it shining plain,
The happy highways where I went
   And cannot come again.

Housman and FitzGerald are, for all their perfection, minor writers. Thomas Hardy is one of the great figures of English literature. We must read his novels to realize his full stature. His poems are often marred by a Browningesque roughness and quaintness. But, to a feeling for the countryside more intimate than Housman's, he joined an extraordinary nobility of spirit. Life to him was essentially tragic; a grim battle, in which man was almost certainly defeated by Fate. Yet he faces it with a brave tender resignation, an unfailing compassion for helpless mortality, which somehow draws the sting from despair. Hardy's clumsy, plaintive strains have a mysterious power to soothe the heart, like the sight of the downland sky he loved so well.

THE END OF THE EPISODE

Indulge no more may we
In this sweet-bitter pastime:
The love-light shines the last time
    Between you, Sweet, and me.

There shall remain no trace
Of what so closely tied us,
And blank as ere love eyed us
    Will be our meeting-place.

The flowers and thymy air,
Will they now miss our coming?
The bumbles thin their humming
    To find we haunt not there?

Though fervent was our vow,
Though ruddily ran our pleasure,
Bliss has fulfilled its measure,
    And see its sentence now.

Ache deep; but make no moans:
Smile out; but still suffer.
The paths of love are rougher
    Than thoroughfares of stones.

Meanwhile, a few poets found security from the prevailing doubt, in the unchanging truths of religious faith. Coventry Patmore and Gerard Hopkins were Catholics. Both were original, unequal writers, whose queer idiosyncrasies make them hard to appreciate at a first reading. Patmore was a follower of Donne, born two hundred years later, whose complex ingenious poetry strives to express a mystical vision mingling sensual and spiritual passion. Hopkins, a Jesuit priest, is difficult not for his thoughts but for his mode of expression. He was always experimenting in language and metre; at times so boldly as to be unintelligible. His successful experiments, however, have a vivid astonishing splendour.

The one great Anglican poet of the period is easy to admire. Rossetti's sister, Christina, expressed simple thoughts in simple language. But she was an inspired genius, in whom an exquisite sense of art was charged by a throbbing passion. Sometimes she sings of love, sometimes of religion; but always with pathetic loveliness. Her modest achievement is one of the most perfect in the whole of English literature.

A BIRTHDAY ·

My heart is like a singing bird
   Whose nest is in a watered shoot;
My heart is like an apple-tree
   Whose boughs are bent with thickset fruit;
My heart is like a rainbow shell
   That paddles in a halcyon sea;
My heart is gladder than all these
   Because my love is come to me.

Other poets with Christian beliefs are also memorable: Francis Thompson, sumptuous and impassioned, and the careful sensitive Alice Meynell.

Meanwhile a few other authors found confidence in life in creeds of their own. Emily Brontë, in a handful of verses, expressed a mysticism as fiery as Blake's; the coloured, complicated poetry of George Meredith proclaimed a belief in the ultimate benevolence of nature; Rudyard Kipling, famous also as a story-teller, made a religion of patriotism. His imaginative appreciation of England's romantic past, his triumphant belief in her imperial destiny, found expression in ringing strains that managed to make themselves heard far beyond the ordinary circles of readers of poetry, and sent their tunes lilting in the heads of Englishmen all over the world.

Finally two writers, living well into the twentieth century, brought Victorian poetry to a close in a fanfare of triumphant music. Their careers run curiously parallel. Robert Bridges, starting as a song writer in a smooth, traditional manner, appeared in his last work, *The Testament of Beauty*, as a philosophic poet, intellectual in subject matter and writing in an austere, highly experimental style; William Butler Yeats made his name as a sort of Irish Rossetti, the author of dreamy moon-lit poems set in a Celtic fairyland. In middle life he deliberately changed his style to become a poet of ideas, severe and rhetorical. Bridges and Yeats both founded their view of life on a belief in the absolute value of their art. They assert their conviction that beauty is its own justification. Here the likeness between them ends. Bridges has a thoroughly English talent combining a fastidious scholarly taste with a fresh birdlike sweetness. The beauty he worships is serene; its classic temple stands in the rich smiling quiet of English park-land.

I love all beauteous things,
  I seek and adore them;
God hath no better praise,
And man in his hasty days
  Is honoured for them.

I too will something make
  And joy in the making;
Altho' to-morrow it seem
Like the empty words of a dream
  Remembered on waking.

Very different is the gleaming shrine of Yeats's adoration, written with the cabalistic symbols of some secret mystery, and shadowed by the boughs of the Irish forest. For all the sophistication of his art, there is something untamed in Yeats's inspiration; for all his mastery of the English tongue, his genius is exotic.

THE NEW FACES

If you, that have grown old, were the first dead,
Neither catalpa tree nor scented lime
Should hear my living feet, nor would I tread
Where we wrought that shall break the teeth of Time.
Let the new faces play what tricks they will
In the old rooms; night can outbalance day,
Our shadows rove the garden gravel still,
The living seem more shadowy than they.

Long before Bridges and Yeats died, poetry had entered on its modern phase. It is beyond the scope of this essay to try and estimate this. The writers of to-day have not been born into a happy age for poetry. The doubt and the despondency of the later nineteenth century have been sharpened for them by the shock of world catastrophe. However, the poets have gone on writing; and though their work is fragmentary compared with that of their predecessors, it is full of originality and life. Individualistic and lyrical, it is still romantic in type. The Georgian poets, who flourished in the first twenty years of the century, were rural romantics. The most typical of them, Edward Thomas, Edmund Blunden and V. Sackville-West, turned away from the unsympathetic atmosphere of industrial England to seek for peace in the homely charms of English country life. Contemporary with them appeared the passionate, disordered rhapsodies of D. H. Lawrence, the sculptured eloquence of Hilaire Belloc, the fresh songs of W. H. Davies, the direct appeal of Masefield's poetry and above all the elfin loveliness of Walter de la Mare.

Half-hidden in a graveyard,
  In the blackness of a yew,
Where never living creature stirs,
  Nor sunbeam pierces through,

Is a tomb-stone, green and crooked –
  Its faded legend gone –
With one rain-worn Cherub's head
  To sing of the unknown.

There, when the dusk is falling,
  Silence broods so deep
It seems that every air that breathes
  Sighs from the fields of sleep.

Day breaks in heedless beauty,
  Kindling each drop of dew,
But unforsaking shadow dwells
  Beneath this lonely yew.

And, all else lost and faded,
  Only this listening head
Keeps with a strange unanswering smile
  Its secret with the dead.

Walter de la Mare

These writers came to maturity before the war of 1914. They still retain something of the serenity of a former age. Even if they were dissatisfied with the world they knew, they felt confidence enough to build a world of their own. Those who felt the shock of the war when still quite young, found this impossible. During the war itself, England produced little poetry; only some poignant verses of hope by Rupert Brooke and others, at the beginning, and at the end some poignant verses of despair by Wilfred Owen and others; these were moving rather from their sincerity of feeling than their poetic excellence.

(right) *Rupert Brooke in 1913: his idealistic war poetry of 1914–15 overshadowed his contribution to the rediscovery of seventeenth-century verse and drama and his interest in Ezra Pound and imagist poetry.*

(opposite) *Edward Thomas in uniform; an etching made in 1915 by John Wheatley. Thomas, like Wilfred Owen and Isaac Rosenberg, was killed in the trenches – an immeasurable loss to English poetry.*

(below) *W. B. Yeats broadcasting for the BBC in about 1936. He was one of the first poets whose reputation was spread by the new media of wireless and gramophone.*

The bleak anti-climax of the peace brought forth a new school led by
T. S. Eliot. These are romantics in full disillusionment, yearning vainly
after ecstasy. Mr Eliot is a Christian; his younger successors, Mr Auden
and Mr Spender, seem to look for salvation to a kind of Communism; but
both are so disheartened that neither the real world nor that of their
dreams seems to give them any zest of inspiration. To express their
frustrated mood they have evolved a new style, complex, intellectual and
ironical, modern in diction, broken in rhythm.

What, at the time of the birth of Our Lord, at Chistmastide,
Is there not peace upon earth, goodwill among men?
The peace of this world is always uncertain, unless men keep the peace of
    God.

And war among men defiles this world, but death in the Lord renews it,
And the world must be cleaned in the winter, or we shall have only
A sour spring, a parched summer, an empty harvest.
Between Christmas and Easter what work shall be done?
The ploughman shall go out in March and turn the same earth
He has turned before, the bird shall sing the same song.
When the leaf is out on the trees, when the elder and may
Burst over the stream, and the air is clear and high,
And voices trill at windows, and children tumble in front of the door,
What work shall have been done, what wrong
Shall the bird's song cover, the green tree cover, what wrong
Shall the fresh earth cover? We wait, and the time is short
But waiting is long.

From Murder in the Cathedral *by T. S. Eliot*

Such poetry is too obscure and too joyless ever to be widely popular. But at its best, it has a pungent fascination, softened by gleams of a wistful beauty. Dorothy Wellesley and W. J. Turner, in their imaginative and philosophical poetry, the Sitwells, Ruth Pitter in her religious verse, have not broken away from the main English tradition. They have contrived to set their modern thought to a music which is still rich with the overtones of past poetry.

Now once more war is sweeping the country. How far it will affect literature and in what direction, it is too early to say. But poetry seems by now so deeply rooted in the English nature, that it is impossible to believe it will ever be extinguished.

Gray's 'Ode on the Death of a Favourite Cat Drowned in a Tub of Gold Fishes';
'What female heart can gold despise? | What cat's averse to fish?' The cat was Walpole's.

EPILOGUE

I wrote the preceding pages over forty years ago. Inevitably they reflect in part the taste of the period in which they were written; also they represent my own literary judgments in an early, immature phase. As such, they must be allowed to stand. But my opinion of some individual authors has since undergone so extreme a change that I feel bound to comment on it. I realize that my whole treatment of what was then contemporary and recent poetry is woefully inadequate: in particular I devote far too little space and praise to Gerard Hopkins and to Edward Thomas, both of whom I have come to regard as among the greatest English writers of the last hundred years.

I want also to say that I have, since I wrote my book, changed my mind about Shakespeare in an important respect. In 1941 I accepted the then conventionally held view that his work lacked a spiritual dimension, that he was not a 'religious' writer: it is true that he tells us nothing about his private personal religion. All the same, more searching examination of his works has convinced me that he is one of the greatest and deepest of Christian writers. *Macbeth* is surely the most impressive expression in our literature of the Christian doctrine of Damnation, and *King Lear* of the Christian doctrine of Redemption; while the full true significance of *Measure for Measure* and *The Winter's Tale*, two of his profoundest works, is only intelligible when interpreted in the light of a specifically Christian and religious vision of reality.

Dramatists

GRAHAM GREENE

ANYONE who goes into a Roman Catholic Church during the Holy Week services, can see for himself the origin of our drama: on Palm Sunday the priest knocks on the door of the church and demands to be admitted, the palms are borne along the aisle: on Good Friday the shrill voices of Judas and the High Priest break into the narrative of the Gospel: the progress to Calvary is made more real by human actors.

It seems a long road to have travelled – from this to the drunken ladies of Noel Coward's *Private Lives*, and one which can only lightly be sketched in so short a book as this. But there remains all the time – whether we are considering the latest farce or the enormous despair of *King Lear* – the sense of ritual. Perhaps the child is more aware of it than the grown man at the theatre: the chatter subdued as the overture begins, or else the three sudden raps like those of the priest at the church door: the regular rise and fall of the curtain between our world and theirs. To the child it little matters what happens upon the stage: the ritual is there – the magic: the maid who crosses the stage towards the ringing telephone as the curtain goes up has to the innocent eye the appearance of an acolyte moving from left to right before the altar.

Even though little evidence is available for the years between it is easy enough to conjecture the way in which the drama began. On one side of the narrow gap is the Mass with its dramatic re-enactment of the Last Supper: on the other the Mystery and Miracle Plays – incidents from the Old and the New Testaments, legends of saints acted often by priests, in the precincts of churches. Popularity drove these plays out of the church into the churchyard where the feet of the mob trampled over the graves. And so to save the graves they had to go further and become more secularized. Acted at fairs on movable scaffolds, forming part of the riotous medieval processions, played by jugglers and members of trade guilds, their subject-matter widened. Noah could be drunk in a market-

Graham Greene, photographed in the early 1960s.

place as he could not be in a church. And so when we look again towards the end of the fifteenth century we find the drama flourishing in nearly a hundred towns, religious still but sometimes twisting into odd Gothic humours. Four great cycles of Miracle Plays (known as the York, Towneley, Chester and Coventry) are still in existence, representing the whole biblical story from the Creation to the Ascension. Of the York cycle we have the order of the Pageant on Corpus Christi, 1415, with each guild assigned its part in the gigantic cycle of the Fall and the Redemption: the Tanners, the Plasterers, Cardmakers, Fitters, Coopers and Armourers, Glovers, Shipwrights, Fishmongers, Bookbinders, Hosiers, Spicers and Pewterers and Chandlers and Vintners – the list is only limited by man's needs. These plays grew, like a church, anonymously: we have reached the drama, but not yet the dramatist.

One reads these plays now for pedantry rather than for pleasure; where humour or a kind of simple poetry creeps in, perhaps we value it too highly for the contrast: the scene in the Chester play of *Noah's Flood* when Noah's wife refuses to enter the ark:

> Yea, sir, sette up youer saile,
> And rowe fourth with evill haile,
> For withouten anye faiyle
>   I will not oute of this towne;
> But I have my gossippes everichone,
> One foote further I will not gone:
> They shall not drowne, by Sante John!
>   And I may save their life.

the scene in *The Sacrifice of Isaac* when Abraham prepares to kill his 'sweet sonne of grace'; or most striking of all – like a comic gargoyle on a Cathedral roof – the *Secunda Pastorum* in the Towneley Plays when just before the Angels sing their *Gloria in Excelsis* we watch the shepherds search the house of Mak, the sheepstealer, and at last find the missing ewe wrapped in swaddling clothes – a bold caricature – lying in a cradle:

> Gyf me lefe hym to kys, and lyft up the clowtt.
> What the deville is this? he has a long snowte.

Alongside the Miracle Play grew up the Morality, of which the story was only the vehicle to illustrate the beauty of virtue and the ugliness of vice. This is the abstract theme of later drama robbed of the particular plot and particular characters – Macbeth appears only as Ambition and Iago

Miracle plays, representations of biblical and saints' stories, were performed throughout England between the twelfth and sixteenth centuries. Four complete cycles presenting the entire biblical scheme survive. Each is associated with a particular town, where the guilds staged a play apiece. This photograph shows a modern revival of the fullest surviving cycle, that of York, performed on a pageant wagon, as in medieval times.

as Deceit. It is the bones without the flesh, just as so often in twentieth-century drama we have the flesh without the bones – characters who act a plot before us and have no significance at all outside the theatre, who are born when the curtain rises and die when it falls.

The Morality play reached its highest point with *Everyman*, composed before the end of the fifteenth century, a play of such permanent interest that it excludes from the attention of all but scholars its predecessors and contemporaries, just as the ordinary man's knowledge of Elizabethan drama is justifiably confined almost entirely to Shakespeare's plays. That it is founded on an original Dutch version is neither here nor there: it lives as poetry and the poetry is English. The plot is as bone-dry and unadorned as the verse: it belongs to the world of the Black Death and the theological argument. God sends Death to Everyman to summon him to judgment, and Everyman's cry, 'O Death, thou comest when I had thee least in mynde', bare and precise and human, goes echoing through the century which separates him from Shakespeare to reappear in the more studied, more evocative, but hardly more telling Renaissance cry: 'She should

Everyman encounters Death; a woodcut from the title-page of a 1530 edition of the most famous of English morality plays, which dramatizes the progress of mankind on earth towards Christian regeneration in the face of death.

have died hereafter. There would have been a time for such a word' – all that fear of death's heavy responsibility which belongs to the Age of Faith and lay on Hamlet's will as much as Everyman's. Everyman tries in vain to bribe Death to delay: but Death is unbribable. He tries to wring out some hope of return. All he can procure is consent that he may take with him a friend on his journey.

And so Everyman goes first to Fellowship, and here under the abstract name we can see the dramatist beginning to evolve character – much as novelists of the eighteenth and nineteenth centuries hid a particular man under the abstract name – Mr Allworthy, Sir Gregory Hardlines and the like. Bluff, cheerful, bogus Fellowship is not quite an abstraction as he greets Everyman: there is nothing he will not do for a friend: only let him name his grief: he will die for him: he will go to Hell for him, but the straight name of Death on his friend's lips freezes his promises.

> Now, by God that all hathe bought,
> If deth were the messenger,
> For no man that is lyvynge todaye
> I will not go that lothe journaye,
> Not for the fader that bygote me.

There is no room to follow Everyman's course in detail: from Fellowship to Good Deeds:

> Here I lye, cold in the grounde,
> Thy synnes hath me sore bounde
> That I can not stire . . .

and on to Knowledge who leads him to Confession, and so to the last sacrament and his farewell to Beauty and Strength, Discretion and the Five Wits, all except Good Deeds. The pilgrimage is conventional, but it is passionately described: it is theologically exact, because that exactitude seemed to the fifteenth-century author to express the truth. It is the first English play that belongs to our living literature, and we have to wait nearly a hundred years for another.

In the interval something new emerges – the author.

These first authors are not of great interest except historically, and that is because the theatre was still the fair and the market-place. To try to revive these plays in a different _milieu_ would be like trying to revive on the great screen, before the huge auditorium of the modern cinema, some little reel of celluloid made for the nickelodeon. The theatre is a popular art, and we must not confuse the historical interest – confined to a few – with the dramatic interest. _Everyman_ lives as poetry, and as a play, but these first experiments in secular drama, by men like Heywood and Bale, have not that much life in their dry bones: Folly, Hypocrisy, Good Deeds and the rest have been given names – they become Johan the Husband, Tyb the Wife, Sir Jhon the Priest, Neighbour Prattle. They have a rough humour, satire as blunt and heavy as a quarter-staff – that applies to Heywood. Bale introduced history – _Kynge Johan_ and _Apius and Virginia_. It is the period of Henry and Mary, when religion is becoming confused with politics, and it is really safer to leave religion alone. Men who write plays have heads to lose and their bodies are as inflammable as others.

The New Learning too had arrived, and simple men, it may well be, were ceasing to write in these confusing times. The unknown authors of the early Miracles were not men of intelligence – they were men of feeling and men who had been taught rather than teachers. The moralities are like children's lessons. The new plays are ceasing to be popular; they are written at Eton for Etonians, acted in colleges and in the Inns of Court, with Terence and Seneca for models, and the stage has become at last stationary – but not in a market-place (though it must be remembered that the mob could still see the old Miracles and Moralities – they were being acted here and there as late as when Hamlet took the stage, just as the Morality, if you look for it, still lingers to-day at the seaside in the Punch booth).

The drama had become separated from the people, and it will not really interest us again until the audience has once more become popular. We are interested in the dramatists of these days only as stations along a line, and we have to go a long way before the line curves and returns towards the market where we started.

So Heywood and Bale are important only as the rude precursors of George Gascoyne and Sackville and Norton, who in turn are only important because they lead us a littler nearer to the day when, without warning, the greatest playwright the world has known broke on his age. Sackville and Norton, whose monstrous _Gorboduc_ (1562) was an exact imitation of Seneca, mark a stage because they were the first to use dramatic blank verse. This new way of writing, the freedom from rhyme, the approach to realism made possible by the broken rhythm, released the dramatic imagination: the speed with which the drama developed from this point is comparable to the speed with which the film developed. How astonishing it is to think that Elizabeth, who listened one January night in 1562 to *Gorboduc* in the Inner Temple Hall, was able to listen forty years later to *Twelfth Night*. Hear the ghosts in that bombed, deserted hall intoning *Gorboduc* before the court:

> We then, alas, the ladies which that time
> Did there attend, seeing that heinous deed,
> And hearing him oft call the wretched name
> Of mother, and to cry to her for aid
> Whose direful hand gave him the mortal wound,
> Pitying – alas, (for nought else could we do),
> His ruthful end, ran to the woeful bed,
> Despoiled straight his breast, and all we might,
> Wiped in vain with napkins next at hand . . .

The instrument had been invented, but who that night could have foretold these sounds from it?

> O, fellow, come, the song we had last night.
> Mark it, Cesario, it is old and plain;
> The spinsters and the knitters in the sun
> And the free maids that weave their thread with bones
> Do use to chant it: it is silly sooth,
> And dallies with the innocence of love,
> Like the old age.

You cannot simply say that Shakespeare was a poet, and that Sackville and Norton were not: the difference to an audience was less subtle than that. These lines of Shakespeare's are *realistic*: they refer to the common known life, they have the uneven rhythm of speech and grammatically they are simple. How difficult by comparison are the involved periods of *Gorboduc*. The audience must often have found themselves hopelessly lost in the maze of those immense rhetorical sentences. They lie over the drama like the folds of a heavy toga impeding movement.

What filled those forty years? One is inclined to answer simply, Marlowe, but of course there were others, hammering at the stiff formal medium, increasing the subject–matter of verse. Religion was better left alone for the time (and afterwards found itself left alone for good) so that Shakespeare only allowed himself occasional glancing lines (Hamlet's

Thomas Kyd's The Spanish Tragedie *(c. 1585) was the hugely successful initiator of the Elizabethan and Jacobean vogue for lurid plays of murder and revenge. In this scene, illustrated on the title-page of the 1615 edition, Hieronimo discovers the body of his son Horatio in an arbour. Horatio's lover, Bel-imperia, struggles with her brother Lorenzo, who is one of the murderers and wears a mask.*

prayer, the papal nuncio rebuking Philip of France) which showed just the fin of the dangerous thoughts moving below the surface. We are still dealing more with the history of verse than of the stage: Kyd, remembered by scholars for *The Spanish Tragedie*, in which the blank verse was constructed with euphuisms as complicated as the dingy plot, but where the play began to lose the bogus dignity of the pseudo-Seneca; Robert Greene who would hardly be remembered to-day if he had not sneered at the young Shakespeare as an 'upstart crow', written a few songs which please anthologists and drunk very deeply; George Peel and Lyly – but they are too many to notice here, these men whose plays only survive in the memory of scholars and enthusiasts. To Greene alone perhaps is this judgment a little unfair: Greene with his idealized milk maids, cool-fingered, spiritual and content, who ranged the air above the dreary room, the alehouse and the stews which formed his actual scene – a scene more pleasing to scholars than to men who live those lives. But even

Greene belongs more to a record of minor poetry than to a record of drama.

We are dealing in this book with dramatists and not with the mechanics of the stage: but it is essential to note in passing the changing _milieu_ – from churchyard to market-place, from market-place to the great household where the peer could watch the players without smelling the vulgar, and from the peer's household, with the support of their patron, into the inn yards. Then in 1576 came the blow which looked like attaching playwrights permanently to the household, when the Corporation of London forbade the performance of plays in public within the bounds for the sake of morality and hygiene. But this was answered in the same year with the first theatre, in Shoreditch, outside the city limits, and so for the first time we get the fixed stage, the management, the responsibility towards the audience, the profit-and-loss account – all those considerations which the dilettante regards as unseemly checks on the freedom of the artist, but which the artist knows to be the very mould of his technique and the challenge to his imagination. It is nothing to wonder at that it took less than thirty years then to produce _Hamlet_, but one may well speculate whether without the commercial theatre the dramatists would ever have risen higher than the learned imitations of Seneca or Terence, or the elaborate and poetic conceits of Lyly.

The result was not immediately seen – even Marlowe did not belong to _his_ stage in the easy way that the miracle players belonged to theirs. Perhaps there is no dramatist more over-rated – and that because his plays are only read and seldom seen. Perhaps it would be wrong to say that _Tamburlaine_ is as unactable as _Philip van Arteveld_ because it has, in its day, been acted, but one detects no enthusiasm even in such classically-minded theatres as the Old Vic for trying the experiment again. Marlowe was a fine poet who can be seen at his best in his translations from Ovid: fine lustful realistic couplets which remind us of Donne's satires. Stray lines from _Dr Faustus_ and _Tamburlaine_ have lodged in the popular memory: the general effect of his work is of a great gallery lit by the sun and lined with statues, hung with pictures, littered by valuable cabinets, tables, _objets d'art_, so many that they end in tedium: the vulgarity of renaissance riches, the over-enjoyment of life, and the concupiscence of a young man. He had immense potentialities which glimmer through the interminable boring rant of _Tamburlaine_ and the broken-backed construction of _Dr Faustus_: in _Edward II_ he came nearer to writing a fine play in which the occasional poetry was conditioned by the action and held in check by character. But he meddled too much in active life: the speculations which brought him a fine for blasphemy were really safer: he was stabbed not, as we used to learn, by a tavern-roisterer, but – as Dr Hotson discovered a few years ago – by a political spy, leaving behind him at the age of twenty-nine a few fine torsos, some mutilated marble. It is always idle to speculate about a dead man's future: a man dies in the way he lives – and Marlowe's life and talent were both spectacular.

He is a telling contrast to his great successor – whom even Greene had sneered at. This is the sort of life we need for great achievement; so anonymous that even rumour runs off the smooth flanks like water: the man who simply works day in, day out, part of the theatre like the boards worn by actors' feet, protectively covered, with no ambition known to his fellows but the one we all can share – of a house and land and security in troubled times. The rumours of unhappy marriage, of a dark mistress and homosexual love, carry the biographer nowhere; nobody who lives escapes a private agony: one can assume them in Shakespeare's case without, like a gossip-writer, fixing the wrong public name. The important thing is the plays, more important even than the poetry, for poetry alone cannot make a good play (or else Tennyson's *Queen Mary*, which contains some of the finest verse he wrote, would live upon the stage).

Obviously, the whole length of this book would be inadequate to deal with one of Shakespeare's plays; let us in the pitiably small space allowed consider this first and greatest Man of the Theatre without looking at the poet. He had, of course, to learn – as no one after him, until we come to the prose Restoration play, had to learn again: he did the work for all. If *Edward II* was the height his predecessors reached, that was little enough for him to build on. Consider these points: how a play begins, how it proceeds and how it ends. What did *Edward II* have to offer to the future then? A good plain opening, it may be said, with Gaveston reading a letter from the King recalling him to England; but from that point we proceed dryly and choppily by chronological stages – like *Little Arthur's History of England* – the meeting with the King, the quarrel with Coventry, the peer's anger, the banishment to Ireland, the recall again to England – all

The Swan Theatre, where Shakespeare and his company performed 1596–7, sketched in about 1596. This copy of an eye-witness drawing by a Dutchman called Johannes de Witt is the only contemporary illustration of the interior of an Elizabethan theatre. The flag, with the Swan device, was flown when a play was being performed.

tectum

porticus

sedelia

orchestra

ingressus

mimorum
aedes.

proscænium.

planities siue arena.

Ex obseruationibus Londinensibus
Iohannis de witt

this compressed shapelessly into a single act which has no unity of itself, where no scene prepares you for the next, without the sense of destiny, the thread on which, rather than the passage of time, a play's scenes should be strung. And what is the play's end? After the horrifying murder of Edward – in which Marlowe's dramatic genius reached its height and the violence of his spirit found for once perfect expression – we have a sorry little hustled postscript in which the young prince – who has hardly been established as a character – turns on the Queen and Mortimer and avenges his father's death. We feel cheated – rather as when the murderer in a detective story proves to be someone who only appears in the last chapter. And how did Marlowe use the chief handicap and – in the right hands – the chief asset of the Elizabethan stage – the absence of scenery? Certainly he improved on *Gorboduc*, whose authors saw in this only an enforced and colourless unity. The scenes of *Tamburlaine*, unlimited by pasteboard sets and an expense-sheet, shifted boldly all over Asia: *Edward II* moved here and there, to London and Warwickshire and Pontefract, but the shifts are never made visible to the audience. The only scene that writes itself on the inner eye is in the bare prison cell, the castle's sewer.

One disparages Marlowe only to throw up into greater relief the craftsmanship of Shakespeare: those first scenes which grip us like the Ancient Mariner's eye – the angry mutterings in the Venice streets, the sudden broil which brings Othello on the scene ('Keep up your bright swords for the dew will rust them'); the witches loitering on the road to Forres; the heroes returning from the field of Troy and passing under Cressida's balcony. The endings: Othello's 'base Indian' lament; Cleopatra's death; the fool's ironical song at the end of *Twelfth Night*; the violence of Hamlet and the sudden close – 'the rest is silence'; the verbal power which continually puts a scene before our eyes far more vividly than the later scene-painters could do it: the dark after-midnight castle where Duncan lies; the forest of Arden; the battlements of Elsinore.

We confuse the issue when we talk of Shakespeare's greatness as a poet: in the plays the poetry is rightness – that is nearly all: the *exact* expression of a mental state; the *exact* description of a scene. 'Think, we had mothers', Troilus's bitter outburst is not poetry in any usually accepted meaning of the word – it is simply the right phrase at the right moment, a mathematical accuracy as if this astonishing man could measure his words against our nature in a balance sensitive to the fraction of a milligramme. The effect it has on our minds is roughly similar to the effect of poetry, but the emphasis on the poetic content of the plays had a disastrous effect on

the future – for it made poets think they were dramatists.   We have left
out of account what the modern dramatist considers most important of all
– character. Of course Shakespeare created characters – Falstaff, Macbeth,
Cressida; but was Hamlet a character, or Lear, or Iago – any more than
Marlowe's Faustus? They are mouthpieces for a mood, for an attitude
to life, far more than characters, and it is doubtful whether in fact
Shakespeare's plays depend on character at all. *Twelfth Night*, his most
perfect play, contains no character; Viola, Olivia, the Duke – they have
just enough of our human nature to play their light lyrical parody of
human emotion; Aguecheek and Sir Toby and Malvolio – these are
fantasies not characters. In that lovely play all is surface. It must be
remembered that we are still within the period of the Morality: they are
being acted yet in the country districts: they had been absorbed by
Shakespeare, just as much as he absorbed the plays of Marlowe, and the
abstraction – the spirit of Revenge (Hamlet), of Jealousy (Othello), of
Ambition (Macbeth), of Ingratitude (Lear), of Passion (Antony and
Cleopatra) – still rules the play. And rightly. Here is the watershed
between the morality and the play of character: the tension between the
two is perfectly kept: there is dialectical perfection. After Shakespeare,
character – which was to have its dramatic triumphs – won a too-costly
victory.

A scene from Shakespeare's Titus Andronicus, *drawn in 1594. Tamora is on her knees,
pleading with Titus for the lives of her two sons, who kneel behind. Aaron the Moor stands
ready with a drawn sword. This is the earliest known illustration to a play of Shakespeare's,
though we do not know whether it represents the play in performance.*

Perhaps the most startling line of poetry in all our literature occurs in one of Shakespeare's sonnets: 'Desiring this man's art, and that man's scope'. Whose scope could the man who wrote both *Twelfth Night* and *Troilus and Cressida* have envied, and whose art? Perhaps the writer who had made poetry realistic envied the conceits of Lyly and Greene: perhaps the creator of Falstaff envied the stiff magnificent dignity of Jonson. We are tempted to the opposite extreme: to be aware only of silence after the burial in Stratford.

But that is unjust to Shakespeare. He had taught the craft of the theatre; he had lifted the play to a level which even without his genius was to remain higher than the one he had found. We have only to compare Jonson's *Sejanus* with the pre-Shakespearian historical plays to notice the difference. The play is less flexible than, say, *Julius Caesar*, dramatically and rhythmically, but what an advance it is on *Edward II*. The blank verse is a little stiff, but is vivid with the sense of life observed from almost the first lines:

> We have no shift of faces, no cleft tongues,
> No soft and glutinous bodies, that can stick
> Like snails on painted walls . . .

In this, Jonson's first play beyond the prentice stage, we notice the quality which reached its height in the great comedies – *Volpone* and *The Alchemist* – the concrete common image – a kind of man-in-the-street poetry:

> . . . which by asserting
> Hath more confirm'd us, than if heart'ning Jove
> Had, from his hundred statues, bid us strike,
> And at the stroke *click'd all his marble thumbs*.

An ex-bricklayer and a braggart who had fought in the Low Countries and killed his man in a duel, the tyrant of a literary group in a favourite inn, he was conscious of his art as no one but Shakespeare had been before him. He might have written Dryden's prefaces – except that his prose was not good enough: he did not believe in happy accidents or fine frenzies – Shakespeare seems all spirit beside his earthly sturdy talent. One admires the quality one lacks, and we know how Jonson admired Shakespeare, but Shakespeare may well have admired in Jonson the sense of huge enjoyment. The sensuality of Volpone or Sir Epicure Mammon is described by a man whom the world has treated well:

Ben Jonson was a bricklayer, soldier and actor before becoming a playwright – experience which he put to good use in his brilliantly constructed comedies, memorable for their depiction of Jacobean low life.

I will have all my beds blown up, not stuft:
Down is too hard: and then, mine oval room
Fill'd with such pictures as Tiberius took
From Elephantis, and dull Aretine
But coldly imitated. Then, my glasses
Cut in more subtle angles, to disperse
And multiply the figures, as I walk
Naked between my succubae . . .

Compare this with those self-torturing lines out of *The Winter's Tale* (a comedy!):

> . . . There have been,
> Or I am much deceived, cuckolds e'er now;
> And many a man there is, even at this present,
> Now while I speak this, holds his wife by th'arm,
> That little thinks she has been sluiced in's absence,
> And his pond fish't by his next neighbour, by
> Sir Smile, his neighbour . . .

or:

> It is a bawdy planet, that will strike
> Where 'tis predominant; and 'tis powerful, think it,
> From east, west, north and south; be it concluded,
> No barricado for a belly . . .

Even to Falstaff Shakespeare gave sombre thoughts, his streaks of pathos; none of Shakespeare's characters belongs to pure comedy – tragedy creeps in with Shylock, with the ageing Falstaff, with a fool's song: heartbreak is always near while 'the worm feeds on the damask cheek'; but the fate of Volpone does not worry us; Jonson alone has presented on the stage the full rich enjoyment of life – this is his real achievement, not his theory of 'humours' which the professors discuss at such length and which he himself considered so important. His range is narrow: nearly all his comedies – and all his best – turn on the humour of the gull and the astute rogue; his verse has not the speed, the vigour, the irregularity of Shakespeare, but he remains the greatest reporter of his age.

The Elizabethan is usually regarded as the richest period of our drama, but it is the Jacobean which saw the greatest plays: the best of Shakespeare and Ben Jonson. Even the minor playwrights had learned the lesson of the master, and none of the smaller Elizabethan fry reached the level of Webster, Massinger, Beaumont and Fletcher, Chapman, even Ford and Tourneur.

There is no space in a book of this size to deal at any length with these authors individually. There was the difficult metaphysical treatment of melodrama which makes Chapman, the author of the two plays of *Bussy D'Ambois* and *The Duke of Biron*, more interesting for the study than the stage, where clarity, directness, speed are necessary; even in his own life, when the taste of the audience was so infinitely superior to that of our own day, he was a failure and could have written with more justice and quite as much pride as Jonson:

> Make not thyself a Page
> To that Strumpet the Stage,
>   But sing high and aloofe,
> Safe from the Wolves black Jaw, and the dull Asses Hoofe.

Far more successful with the Jacobean audience were the romantic pair, Beaumont and Fletcher, who handed on the theme of Honour to Dryden and the Restoration tragedians in plays packed to absurdity with scruples; even the best, *The Maid's Tragedy*, contains situations as grotesquely unreal as when Aspasia dresses in boy's clothes and incites her faithless lover to a duel so that she may die by his hands. Yet the plays are saved by a youthful lyricism as fresh as the Elizabethan and less conceited, with a charming sensuous sexuality which makes the marriage preparations in *The Maid's Tragedy* as free from offence as Spenser's *Epithalamion*. Of all these dramatists Webster stands alone by virtue of his one great play, *The Duchess of Malfi*, the only play of which it is possible to say that, owing nothing to Shakespeare, it yet stands on a level with the great tragedies. *The White Devil* had showed him to be a poet of some erratic genius: it alone would have left a memory of morbid and magnificent lines: we should have remembered him with Ford and Tourneur, a group who share a kind of dark horror, a violent moral anarchy which seems to have followed the Elizabethan age like a headache after a feast. Among these writers you are aware of no moral centre, no standard of moral criticism – your hero may be an incestuous murderer, the most moving lines may be put in the mouth of an adulteress who has plotted the murder of her husband. In *King Lear* the cruelty of the world may appal us, but somewhere outside there is virtue: the seventeenth century is not eternity, and death is an escape and not an end. But in Tourneur and the earlier Webster we are in the company of men who would really seem to have been lost in the dark night of the soul if they had had enough religious sense to feel despair: the world is all there is, and the world is violent, mad, miserable and without point. The religious revolution had had its effect: this was the rough uneasy strait which led to the serene Anglicanism of Herbert and Vaughan, and to the sceptical doldrums of the eighteenth century: in between the old unquestioning faith and the new toleration lay an unhappy atheism, which has none of the youthful rebelliousness of Marlowe's:

> We are merely the stars' tennis balls, struck and bandied
> Which way please them.

That attitude carried to Tourneur's extreme cannot make a good play, though it can make great poetry. Put on the lowest grounds – an audience must know whom to clap and whom to hiss. Webster's Vittoria Corombona, conceived as a devil, is transformed by the poetry of the trial scene into a heroine – it is too confusing.

But Webster emerged. Bosolo, the self-tortured tool of the Duchess of Malfi's brothers, has the bitter voice of an exile who has not quite forgotten. In his despair he uses heavenly images:

> What's this flesh? a little crudded milk, fantastical puff paste. Our bodies are weaker than those paper prisons boys use to keep flies in; more comtemptible, since ours is to preserve earthworms. Didst thou ever see a lark in a cage? Such is the soul in the body: this world is like her little turf of grass, and the Heav'n o'er our heads, like her looking glass, only gives us a miserable knowledge of the small compass of our prison.

An exile who has not quite forgotten, a prisoner who knows by his own fate that there is such a thing as liberty – that is why Webster is an incomparably finer dramatist than Tourneur. He emerges in his later play far enough from the darkened intellectual world to organize – Vittoria Corombona speaks with the voice of angels, but the Duchess of Malfi is on the side of the angels. And on the side too, of ordinary commonplace humanity. Nowhere among this group of dramatists – except fleetingly in Ford – will you find the note of recognizable everyday tenderness as you find it in Webster, in the love scene when the Duchess gently forces Antonio to declare his love. It is as if the dark Jacobean vapours are lifting, and almost anything might have been expected of Webster if he had not died. Alone of these men he left behind something essentially his: only a scholar could differentiate between untitled scraps of the other poets, but Webster's tone is unmistakable – the keen, economical, pointed oddity of the dialogue – whether in prose or verse – expressing the night side of life:

> How tedious is a guilty conscience.
> When I look into the fishpond in my garden,
> Methinks I see a thing armed with a rake
> That seems to strike at me.

In this one respect his power was greater than Shakespeare's. That enormous genius must be allowed his limitations; even in his darkest period he was too sane, too conscious of his art, to express madness convincingly. The mad Lear is no more mad than Hamlet – he is only distraught, and Ophelia and her flowers is a pretty conceit that might have come from one of Greene's novels. Surrealism is an overworked and a dubious term, but an intellectual generation which has re-discovered Blake and wandered with Dedalus and Bloom through the Dublin night should be quick to recognize the quality of Webster:

> Woe to the caroche that brought home my wife from the masque at three o'clock in the morning! It had a large feather bed in it.

The astonishing thing is not that Webster has so small a public to-day but that he once had so large a one, the great popular audiences of the playhouse – this was what going to the play meant then that to-day means watching a Van Druten, a St John Ervine or a Dodie Smith.

The enormous tide ebbed, and it was nearly fifty years before the English theatre produced another man of genius; a few names are left on the beach for scholars to pore over – Shirley, known to everyone for his lyric, 'The Glories of our Blood and State', from *Ajax and Ulysses*; Suckling, whose *Ballad of a Wedding* is worth all his tedious blank verse plays; and Sir William Davenant, a fine lyric writer but an indifferent playwright, though he claimed to be Shakespeare's bastard (is the story too well known to repeat here of the priest who met the child Davenant running up Oxford High Street towards the Turl where he lived, and asked him what was the hurry? He replied that his godfather Shakespeare had come, to which the priest replied, 'Why do you take the name of God in vain?' The tale is Davenant's own).

The moon which drew the tide back was civil war, the triumph of the Puritans. The theatres had always had a precarious existence: now they stopped altogether. The Puritan spirit ruled the country as much as the town: there were no longer any bounds beyond which the theatre could migrate: the market place as a centre of enjoyment had ceased to exist and the day of the miracle play was at last done. Men began to write plays to be read only: the literary quality of dialogue became more important than the dramatic: life was extinguished between calf boards.

It is wrong to think of the years of the Civil War and the Protectorate as an interlude merely between two dramatic periods – the closing of the theatres had as permanent an effect on our literature as the beheading of a king had on our constitution. The theatre had begun by being popular, had become a 'class' entertainment and then become popular again; now it ceased to be anything but the recreation of the educated, the aristocratic, and later, when these two terms ceased to be synonymous, of the well-to-do. The people were to disappear – or to become a few rude voices from the gallery reported in the Press with disapproval after a First Night. Most of us have been present on some occasion of baffled dislike among the 'Gods' – courtesy title like that given to Prime Ministers after the power has gone: the hisses and catcalls from the gallery are drowned by the claps from the stalls, who feel that the author in some mysterious way belongs to them.

And belong he does. The Puritans saw to that. Shakespeare had belonged to the people, catching for the first time in verse the accent of common speech, giving them the violent, universal tragedies they understood – Doll Tearsheet and the murderer's knife and the laughter of clowns, and of course so much more: Jonson, too, had belonged to them, with his broad realism and downright poetry. They had served the people and the people had moulded them. The frequenters of bear-baiting demanded vitality: men and women who had watched from their windows the awful ritual of the scaffold were ready for any depth of horror the playwright cared to measure.

But when the play returned, it returned almost literally to the drawing-room. There are always ways of evading authority if men care enough, and men have always cared deeply for storytelling. Perhaps if a novelist of Fielding's stature had been alive then, the play would never have flared into brief life, but the long folio romances translated from the French and Spanish must always have been a rather poor substitute for something better. So Davenant brought the play cunningly back by way of a mixed entertainment given in private – something rather like a revue with satirical dialogue and a few songs and some music.

That private atmosphere remained. When the theatres reopened – for a long while there were only two of them – the public were almost as much excluded as they had been at Davenant's entertainments. Tragedies like Dryden's *The Conquest of Granada*, written on the Corneille model in heroic couplets, with their complex ideals of honour, their exaggerated unities, their exalted sentiments and complete lack of human passion, were for the educated who could judge the technical dexterity of the verse, for the enforced travellers of the Court who could appreciate the echoes of what they had heard on the Continent.

Little wonder that it was, in these court circles, a time for foreign fashions: England had given these men nothing more attractive than prison, exile, impoverishment and prudery. Tuke's blank verse romance, *The Adventure of Five Hours*, was the first great success of the new theatre – with the Court: the poor, in the theatrical eye, did not exist, and when the bourgeois began reluctantly to enter the playhouse it was to see himself mocked, for he was now of the losing party: the City had sided with Parliament, and the cuckolds and wanton city wives and leanshanked aldermen of Restoration drama represented a kind of civilized vengeance for the scaffold at Whitehall. Compare Jonson's prose comedy, *Bartholomew Fair*, with Shadwell's *Epsom Fair*, and you notice two things: improvement in the prose and a narrowing in the scope. Jonson was writing about human nature for a public as wide as his subject: the Restoration dramatist with his infinitely more graceful instrument was fashioning an amusing bijou for the drawing-room – a witty and scandalous joke against an unpopular and rather stupid neighbour. That, of course, is to ignore Restoration tragedy, but except for a handful of plays by perhaps three authors it deserves to be ignored.

Comedy before the Restoration had been poetic, and the new comedy does on occasion reach the level of poetry. Dryden's *Marriage à la Mode*, Wycherley's *Country Wife*, Cowley's *Cutter of Coleman Street*, even 'starched Johnie Crowne's' *Country Wit* and the best of Etherege build up a seacoast of Bohemia where rakes talk with the tongues of poets. You can name these plays in the same sentence as *Twelfth Night*; the sweet sound that breathes upon a bank of violets breathes just as sweetly through the curtains of the great four-poster. And yet something has disappeared for ever: Southwark and Bankside are no longer there. *The Country Wife*, the lovely nonsense tale of the man who spread the rumour of his own impotency so that all the husbands in town left the field open to him for grazing in, is perhaps the finest prose comedy in our language. But it was not only among the dull staid citizens of the Exchange that the subtle obscenities of Mr Horner and Lady Fidget failed to find appreciation – the rough Elizabethan mob had had another name for 'china', and something went out of our literature when society took over the theatres.

The social reign lasted roughly forty years – from the Restoration of Charles II to the death of Dryden, and it is dominated by that great unlovable coffee-house figure. Other men wrote single plays of greater genius, but Dryden organized his age; he led it through the period of the heroic tragedy in couplets back to blank verse which was almost free of the Shakespearian echo, led it into the amusing parochial morass of Restoration comedy, then publicly apologized and washed his hands and led it out again towards respectability and Sheridan. And like Jonson – and unlike most of his contemporaries – he knew exactly what he was doing: his critical essays – the first example of really modern prose – blazed the way he had gone. He made the prose-play just as surely as Shakespeare made the poetic: his contemporaries may have mocked the long critical prefaces, but they accepted the standards of taste he laid down, and to a great extent we can accept them still. Aristotle dates more than Dryden. The theatre he left behind was the modern theatre even in its mechanics – the scenery, the shape of the stage. If we leave Shakespeare out of account there is no period of our dramatic literature equal to the Restoration. Pampered and artificial, appealing to the educated few, lacking in moral interest, it was yet superbly finished. Wycherley, Etherege, Aphra Behn, Sedley, even Crowne produced plays which would hold the stage now as securely as *The Importance of Being Earnest* if it were not for the conventions of modern production: these plays need acting in modern clothes far more than Shakespeare's: the monstrous wig, the elegant cane, the flutter of lace handkerchiefs disguise their speed and agility.

Always in the foreground is Dryden, the great Mogul: wringing poetry even out of heroic tragedy with its flattery of human nature: then contemptuously abandoning the forms he had himself established to men like Elkanah Settle, the political hack who ended his days as part of the dragon at Bartholomew Fair; planting in *Marriage à la Mode* the seed which was to flower in *The Country Wife*: already detaching himself from the obscene convention by the time Jeremy Collier launched his attack on the immorality of the stage, and in *All for Love* and *Don Sebastian* writing the last tragedies in blank verse which were to hold the stage for longer than their age. He was, as I have said, the great organizer, and the dramatic period that followed the Jacobean needed organization. It had its own darkness and its own anarchy, a flippant instead of a poetic anarchy. It is impossible to separate life and literature. Dryden almost alone among the writers of his time was ruled by an idea – the idea of authority. There is no inconsistency in his praise of Cromwell and his welcome to Charles: William he never welcomed, for by that time he had found the source of his idea and become a Catholic. Among the lechers and stoics of his time

This scene from The Empress of Morocco *(1673) by the prolific tragedian Elkanah Settle, in performance at the Duke's Theatre, London, shows the new elaborate scenic effects of the Restoration theatre.*

he stands as a figure of astonishing sanity: he was never taken in. One remembers the lines in *Don Sebastian* which compare the tempting stoical ideal of suicide with the Christian:

> But we like sentries are obliged to stand
> In starless nights and wait th' appointed hour.

The idea did not always make for perfect plays. In *The Spanish Friar*, for instance, one is aware of more thought in the background than the thin plot will stand. He produced nothing so graceful or perfect in form as

Wycherley (apart from *Marriage à la Mode* most of the comedies are trivial enough, though lightened by incomparable lyrics); he had not the vitality in comedy of the despised Shadwell (and perhaps that was one reason for fastening a caricature of that gross figure before the eye of posterity); he had not perhaps – with all his logic, precision and steady growth in religious conviction – the moral genius of poor Nathaniel Lee who died in Bedlam, author of *The Princess of Cleves*, a strange Jacobean echo, but his leadership of the stage could hardly be questioned even by his enemies – who lampooned him and on one occasion set hired bravos to cudgel him as he left his coffee-house. The only man posterity has oddly enough chosen to set beside him is Otway, who, like Lee, died young and miserably. *Venice Preserved*, its blank verse written with ponderous regularity, hardly justifies his reputation. Perhaps the caricature of Shaftesbury has helped to give the play a longer life : scholars often like a little lubricity as a change from detective stories. Otway deserves to be remembered better for *The Soldier's Fortune*, a prose comedy which ranks only just below Wycherley.

Into this by no means happy company of playwrights – engaged in ferocious internecine intrigues reflected in the satires of Dryden and Rochester – Jeremy Collier was to burst with his too successful diatribe. It was as if the sense of humour had died with Charles. There followed three years of a moral stupid monarchy stiff and stubborn with the knowledge of other men's mockery, and then the Dutchman whose private life was too dubious even for lampooning was to become with his neglected queen an emblem of middle-class respectability. Dryden, Otway, Wycherley, Etherege, Shadwell, Crowne, Sedley and Behn: these in certain plays reached the height of intellectual comedy – their successors with three exceptions were only shadows. The exceptions were Vanbrugh, Farquhar and Congreve.

Vanbrugh carried on the tradition of Shadwell and Crowne – in between building those immense blocks of stone which are like the magnificent tombs of domestic greatness. His plays are on the old pattern with stupid country knights born for cuckoldry : his personal contribution

David Garrick as Sir John Brute in an eighteenth-century revival of Colley Cibber's version of Vanbrugh's comedy The Provok'd Wife. *Garrick first played Brute in 1774; the part was one of his greatest triumphs. The drunken Brute has put on a dress intended for his wife; the painting (by Zoffany) shows him defying the Watch which is attempting to arrest him: 'Sirrah, I am Bonducca, Queen of the Welchmen . . .'.*

was a knowledge of life which went further than the Court, the coffee-house, the New Exchange and the plays of his contemporaries – a breath of the active world and the wars in Flanders. As for Congreve, Dryden began the long tradition of overpraise. He had already handed on his laurels to several other poets before, in 1694, he wrote his lines, 'To My Dear Friend, Mr Congreve, on his Comedy called The Double Dealer':

> In Him all Beauties of this Age we see;
> Etherege his Courtship, Southern's Purity,
> The Satyre, Wit and Strength of Manly Wycherley . . .

reaching the astonishing conclusion:

> Heav'n, that but once was Prodigal before,
> To Shakespeare gave as much; she could not give him more.

The Way of the World, in which Congreve's thin and perfect talent neatly and beautifully expired 'like the rose in aromatic pain', will always be the delight of the dilettante – it is the dizziest height to which an amateur author has ever climbed. Congreve, as we know from the famous meeting with Voltaire, considered himself a gentleman rather than an author; that is why his plays remain only exquisitely worded imitations of rougher work. He contributed nothing new to the stage: the famous scene in which Millamant lays down her conditions for marriage was a polished repetition of innumerable similar scenes. Even those famous lines which describe the approach of Millamant remind us of other lines by a far greater poet – to Delilah:

> With all her bravery on, and tackle trim,
> Sails fill'd, and streamers waving . . .

Poor despised Crowne, in *The Country Wit*, had provided as good situations: Shadwell had had more life, and Wycherley more stagecraft – Congreve, like the smooth schoolboy, stole the prize and remains in most people's eyes the pattern-writer of Restoration comedy.

Farquhar followed one of the fashions of his time in dying young, leaving, at the age of thirty, seven plays behind, of which *The Recruiting Officer* and *The Beaux' Stratagem* are the most successful. This was the last fling of real Restoration comedy before Sentiment completely won the day, and Farquhar has a touch of genuine feeling, of wider poetry, and of the hurly-burly of experience which his predecessors lacked. *The Beaux'*

Stratagem is the kind of play which Fielding might have written if all his serious attention had not been given to the novel – the lovely opening in the sleepy inn with the bustle of the night coach, the unctuous innkeeper, the pretty daughter, the gentlemen of the road, and the gibbet and the horse-pistols in the background of the comedy – as if Tom Jones and Jonathan Wild had got between the same covers with the hilarity a little subdued at the approach of death (Farquhar was dying as he wrote). The satire is more human than Wycherley's, who was concerned with man only as a grotesque sexual animal, and the lyricism Etherege might have envied: above all there is a masculinity: 'Give me a Man that keeps his Five Senses keen and bright as his Sword'; the fortune hunter boasts when he pools his resources with his friend in pursuit of an heiress: 'I am for venturing one of the hundreds if you will upon this Knight-Errantry; but in case it should fail, we'll reserve the t'other to carry us to some Counterscarp, where we may die as we liv'd in a Blaze.'

So long as Farquhar, Congreve and Vanbrugh lived, prose was still written for the stage with the wit and unexpectedness of poetry. When we hear of the dull-witted husband who 'comes flounce into Bed, dead as a Salmon into a Fishmonger's Basket', we are still not so far from Shakespeare and Jonson. The sense of ritual has not been lost, for ritual is the representation of something real abstracted from any individual element. It is the common touch in the human portrait – Cromwell without the personal eccentricity of the warts. Lady Fidget, it is true, is more of a 'character' than Lady Macbeth, but she is still sufficiently abstracted – silly charming Wantonness itself passes across the stage as in a Morality and not a particular woman. All good dramatic prose – or poetry – has this abstract quality, by which, of course, I do not mean a woolliness, a vagueness. On the contrary the abstract word is the most concrete. But now the great period has drawn to a close. You will notice how often the writers of comedy as well as of tragedy up to now have had as their main figures representations of the dark side of human nature – Volpone, Shylock, Mr Horner. Now sentiment is going to creep in: the author is going to fall in love with his own creations, identify himself with them, flatter himself by endowing them with all kinds of winning traits, so that we shall no longer watch Avarice, Lust, Revenge, Folly meeting the kind of fate which satisfies our sense of destiny. The happy ending is here, and we shall listen to Addison winning moral approval with the empty words of Cato, or Goldsmith's Mr Hardcastle uttering the smug sentiments which will endear the author to his audience: 'I love

William Congreve (1670–1729). His great comedies, all written before 1700, were at the time less enthusiastically received than his now-forgotten tragedy, The Mourning Bride *(1697).*

everything that's old: old friends, old times, old manners, old books, old wine; and I believe, Dorothy, you'll own I have been pretty fond of an old wife.' A generation before, sentiments like those could only have been uttered satirically. Now the author's personality has begun to shoulder his characters aside. We have reached the end of serious dramatic writing: only individual authors will break the general barrenness.

The high points of eighteenth-century drama are usually regarded as these: *The School for Scandal, The Rivals, She Stoops to Conquer*. It must be admitted that Sheridan and Goldsmith have held the stage, if it is enough to secure year by year the compulsory attendance of school children at well-meaning matinees. The awful humours of the duel scene in *The Rivals*, Lady Teazle 'm'ludding' and flirting a fan, the unconvincing villainies of Joseph Surface, the sentimentalities of Mr Hardcastle, Mrs Malaprop's repetitive errors – have they really delighted generations or is it only that they have been considered safe plays for young people –

Restoration comedy without the sex? Sheridan's style has the smooth unoriginal proficiency of a Parliamentary orator: Congreve lacks life but he sparkles beside his successor. There is no reason why Sheridan should have been thus preferred to such minor writers as Mrs Centlivre – except that her humour was still a little dubious, or George Colman, whose comedy, *The Jealous Wife*, does possess a certain tang – the atmosphere of stables and Smithfield inns: it was simply that Sheridan was a personality, and he traded himself successfully. Authors were no longer so anonymous that the researches of scholars unearth only a few bills, a doubtful signature, or an unimportant law suit.

As for Goldsmith, his success was assured as soon as the age of Nell Gwyn and Moll Davis was over. The bourgeois, who had been the butt of the theatre, ruled the stalls and boxes: respectability must be the hero now,

The auction scene from Sheridan's The School for Scandal, *first performed at Drury Lane Theatre, London, in 1777. The improvident but kind-hearted Charles Surface sells off his family portraits, unaware that the purchaser is his uncle, intent on discovering which of his two nephews – Charles or the apparently virtuous Joseph – should become his heir.*

and if a Lady Fidget were to appear at all she must be treated with solemn reprobation. Marriage is no longer the subject of a joke: it is the happy ending to which all plays tend. Typical of the period is Arthur Murphy's *The Way to Keep Him*, in which two husbands for five acts remain secretly in love with their own wives: these plays usually end with little tags – one cannot call them moral so much as conventional. 'In my opinion,' Murphy brings down the curtain, 'were the business of this day to go abroad into the world, it would prove a very useful lesson: the men would see how their passions may carry them into the danger of wounding the bosom of a friend' (O, the shades of Mr Horner!) 'and the ladies would learn that, after the marriage rites are performed, they ought not to suffer their powers of pleasing to languish away, but should still remember to sacrifice to the Graces.' It sounds more like the subject for a ladies' magazine article than a play. Compare that discreet admonitory curtain with the old comedy, with the fool singing, 'For the rain it raineth every day'. It was the period of blarney: Sheridan, Goldsmith, Murphy – what a lot of Irishmen from that time forth were to make a good living out of the easily pleased prosperous public of the English theatre. They all had a certain flair – Murphy could turn a phrase quite as adequately as Sheridan: here was the touch of wistful poetry – 'Adieu for him the sidebox whisper, the soft assignation, and all the joys of freedom': a certain wit – 'She has touched the cash; I can see the banknotes sparkling in her eyes', and an occasional piece of vivid and robust reporting:

> Did I not go into Parliament to please you? Did I not go down to the Borough of Smoke-and-Sot, and get drunk there for a whole month together? Did I not get mobbed at the George and Vulture? And pelted and horsewhipped the day before the election? And was not I obliged to steal out of the town in a rabbit-cart? And all this to be somebody as you call it? Did not I stand up in the House to make a speech to show what an Orator you had married? And did not I expose myself? Did I know whether I stood upon my head or my heels for half an hour together? And did not a great man from the Treasury Bench tell me never to speak again?

Indeed men like Murphy had a great deal of talent: they had not the dreadful melting tenderness of Goldsmith or the smoothness of Sheridan, but it is the plot now and not the theme that matters. The illustration of the idea has driven the idea itself out of the theatre. We are beginning to ask the question, 'How can he get five acts out of that?' A question which never troubled an earlier audience. It is a question which becomes increasingly troublesome the nearer we get to the persons of the play; the less abstract the drama the more we identify ourselves with the drama. Jealousy and Passion can fill any number of acts, but the misadventures of George and Margaret cannot.

One man there was with a more robust talent, and that was Foot, the comic actor-playwright, who has been called, rather unwisely, the English Aristophanes. He cannot stand up to a term like that: racy and vigorous though his plays are, we have to use the historic sense to appreciate them, for they depend for their interest on personalities who are now buried in the footnotes of history. He did in the theatre what Rowlandson did in painting, but the paintings have outlived the plays.

The trouble was – we had been too fortunate in our drama. Not even France could boast the equal of our greatest names. With the works of Shakespeare, Jonson and Dryden to draw upon, managers found it unnecessary to encourage fresh talent. And of course it was much cheaper. Mr W. D. Taylor has calculated that 'of the thirteen parts Garrick chose to appear in during his farewell performances at the beginning of 1776, ten are from plays written before 1730', and the same critic has noted a secondary cause of decline: 'The greatest geniuses of the century preferred the novel. Neither Defoe nor Richardson nor Smollett nor Sterne attempted the dramatic form.' Though, in fact, Smollett did.

The theatre was not to see a revival until new subject-matter attracted better brains. The old abstract drama had dealt with important things: with 'the base Indian who threw a pearl away richer than all his tribe', with the lark in the cage and the soul in the body; that had gone, perhaps for ever, and the theatre had become a kind of supplement to *The Ladies' Magazine*. The religious sense was at its lowest ebb, and the political did not exist as we know it to-day. Man's interests shrank like a rockpool in the hard bright sunlight of reason. Garrick rewrote Shakespeare. (So in a small way had Davenant and Dryden, but at least they were fellow-poets: Garrick was one of the new breed of theatrical business men – the actor-managers.)

The new subject-matter therefore could not be abstract and poetic: it had to be realistic, but on a different plane of realism. It had to be important as a leading article may be important, deal with ideas important for the period if it could not deal with ideas important for all periods. Tom Robertson's *Caste*, produced in 1867, is usually held to mark the change. It is not a play which bears revival: stilted and melodramatic, it was conventional enough in everything but the one novelty, that it did state, though in primitive naïve terms, the economic and social facts: as its finest flower it was to seed the work of Pinero, Henry Arthur Jones, Galsworthy, dramatists whose plays have barely outlived their deaths.

It was the first self-seeding in the English theatre since the days of the Miracle play. Always before the seed had blown from abroad – as it was to do again at the end of the century. From Spain and France we had magnificently developed. In our own island we were shut in: there was not the intellectual room to breathe, and the absence of foreign influences in the greater part of the nineteenth century – due perhaps in part to Victorian complacency, for did not we lead the world in coal and steam and were not foreigners notoriously immoral? – had an odd and interesting effect. The theatre may sometimes appear dead, but it cannot die, and the English theatre developed in the empty years strange freaks to hold the attention. Many of these were imported from the Continent, but you can hardly dignify them by the name of influences. Our greatest actors ranted about the stage listening to imaginary bells, or mounted the scaffold as Sidney Carton – 'It is a far, far better thing . . .'. It was as if a buried popular public were signalling desperately for release: as if we were on the verge of rediscovering through the crudest melodrama a popular poetry. But middle-class educated opinion was too strong.

This was the age when the producer came into his own. And the designer. Scenery had never been so important since the days of the seventeenth-century masque, but it was painfully realistic scenery. Soon we would be reading 'Cigarettes by Abdullah. Vacuum cleaner in Act 2 by the Hoover Company.' The Times Furnishing Company is on the horizon, and soon we would be reading of Miss So-and-so's dresses and who had made them. *Caste* had given quite a new turn to triviality.

There were attempts at better things as the century progressed – attempts which beat hopelessly against the realistic tide. There was Tennyson's *Queen Mary* and Browning's *Strafford*. But the poets were too long-winded now that they wrote to be read, and the actor-managers who produced their plays smothered their merits under the expensive costumes. Browning had a real sense of the stage. *Pippa Passes* shows what a dramatist he might have been if the audience had been there, for audiences get the dramatists they deserve (if only the critics who sneer at the bear-baiting public of Shakespeare would remember that). The quick love scene between Ottima and Sebald the first dawn after they have done away with the old doting husband is worthy of the Jacobeans – Sebald's shuddering refusal of *red* wine and Ottima's cry when conscience and despair drive them to suicide: 'Not to me, God – to him be merciful.' Browning, living in Italy, was free from the prudery of his age: he could afford to be honest: and his dramatic verse has the magnificent voluptuousness of a better time – 'Those morbid, olive, faultless shoulder-blades'. Tennyson, too, in *Queen Mary*, nearly wrote a great play. But he was hemmed in by indifference: in that prosperous and realistic age you could not deal effectively with the subtlety and the cruelty of religion. *Queen Mary* was stifled in its conception by the worldly success of the Church of England.

But these plays were as much 'sports' in the Victorian theatre as Yeats's in the Edwardian, or Flecker's *Hassan*, or Eliot's *Murder in the Cathedral* in our own. The three-act play was here: the drawing-room set, the library set, and after a few more years the bedroom set. Cigarette cases were being offered, and very soon now butlers and parlour-maids would be crossing the stage, as the curtain rose, to answer the telephone. The panelling in the library looks quite Tudor, the club is lifted straight from St James's (and now that acting has become a respectable profession the actors can be lifted from there, too).

There was something new in this: the novelty of photography – which was also to be mistaken for an art. Technically the new writers were amazingly accomplished. The theatre had become very slipshod: the soliloquy, a very valuable convention, had become hopelessly debased, and the aside, for which there was never very much to be said, had multiplied to such an extent that almost half the play of a dramatist of Murphy's time was addressed to the audience. Pinero and Jones levelled the play up against everyday behaviour and snipped off the excrescences. Nowadays, these plays have almost an old-fashioned charm: they join Mrs Cameron's photographs among the period pieces, but that only goes to show how up-to-the-minute they were in their own day – up-to-the-minute even in their conventionalities. The sentimentality of *London Pride* may be a little overwhelming – but so is the sentimentality of Mr Noël Coward's *Design for Living*; we don't recognize sentimentality until it has dated a little. These writers, too, were daring: *The Second Mrs Tanqueray*, melodramatic and sentimental though it seems now, marked an advance as great as *Caste*: sexual situations could now be presented seriously in prose if they avoided crudities likely to offend the Lord Chamberlain, just as many years later Galsworthy's *Silver Box* was to open the way to criticism of our institutions. This type of play was to reach its apotheosis in Mr Granville-Barker's *Waste*, in which we are convincingly introduced to the private lives of Cabinet Ministers. Church disestablishment is discussed at a length that only a consummate craftsman could have made tolerable; the theme is the social convention that enforces the resignation of a Member of Parliament who is co-respondent in a divorce suit: the title of course refers to the waste involved in the retirement of the one Minister capable of nursing through Parliament the Disestablishment Bill. Mr Barker might have written a play about Parnell, but he chose deliberately the rather drab political issue, just as Henry James in his later novels chose ugly names for his heroines: above all there must be no fortuitous glamour to confuse the subject with the plot. No other play of the realistic school is so likely to survive the circumstances of its time. It is honest through and through, and it is without a trace of the sentimentality that betrayed Galsworthy.

There was, of course, bound sooner or later to be a reaction against this sober high-minded pattern. Dryden, it was said, found English prose brick and left it marble: these authors were certainly remaking it in rather ugly bricks like a workhouse wall. One bright spirit had evaded capture, leaving behind him, after he had died of drink and disease, one of the most

Mrs Patrick Alexander as Paula and George Alexander as Aubrey Tanqueray in Arthur Wing Pinero's The Second Mrs Tanqueray *(1893). The play, which deals with the marriage of a respectable widower to a social outcast – a woman with 'a past' – was considered daring and controversial at the time.*

(left) *Oscar Wilde in New York in 1882. On his arrival he announced: 'I have nothing to declare except my genius.'*

(right) *Allan Aynesworth as Algernon Moncrieff and George Alexander as John Worthing in the first production of Wilde's 'trivial comedy for serious people',* The Importance of Being Earnest *(1895). Algernon is an unwelcome visitor to John Worthing's country home; having fascinated Cecily, John's ward, he is now eating all the muffins.*

perfect plays in our theatre. How beautifully free from any sense of period at all is Wilde's *Importance of Being Earnest*. In *Lady Windermere's Fan* he tried to play the game like his contemporaries, but he had not their sense of reality and the result was rather like an Academy problem picture, but in *The Importance* he shook off his age and soared as freely in the delirious air of nonsense as Edward Lear.

Meanwhile, with critics like Mr Bernard Shaw and William Archer in the stalls, a certain depression over the North Sea was bound to strike our

The leading dramatists of the Edwardian stage: from left, J. M. Barrie, John Galsworthy, George Bernard Shaw and Harley Granville-Barker.

shores. Henry James mercilessly described the atmosphere of Ibsen's plays as 'an odour of spiritual paraffin'; the long Oslo winter and the light of oil lamps had helped to form these extraordinary plays in which town councillors and sanitary inspectors wrestled with their egos as ferociously as the Prince of Denmark in surroundings of appalling drabness. To audiences accustomed to Pinero these plays were inexpressibly odd and obscure: factions developed, with critics in opposing camps: the cause was not helped by Archer's creaking translations. *The Doll's House* had a comparatively easy passage: 'women's rights' was a subject even Pinero might have tackled, but *The Master Builder, The Wild Duck* – this mixture of poetic symbolism and realistic detail could not be understood by that generation. It was as strange to Shakespeare lovers as to Pinero 'fans'. And before they had really time to accept Ibsen a second northern depression reached our island, this time from Russia; and the Stage Society produced Tchekhov.

But Pinero, Jones and, increasingly, Galsworthy, and later Maugham, remained the staple fare, though perhaps the general shaking-up by Ibsen and Tchekhov caused as near an approach to passionate approval and fanatical disapproval as the English public could express, and helped the success of two authors who stood right outside the realistic social convention – Shaw and Barrie. Ibsen had introduced intellectual discussion to the stage, and Shaw seized his opportunity; though perhaps it is too fantastic to detect a resemblance between the frustrated hopes, the wistful dreams and the strangely natural behaviour of Tchekhov's characters and Barrie's fairy backgrounds, enchanted woods, and Never Neverlands.

It would be idle here to attempt to scratch the tough surface of Mr Shaw's enormous world-wide reputation. With Wilde, Byron, Galsworthy and Edgar Wallace he is the representative of our literature on the Continent. Like Sterne, another Irishman, he plays the fool at enormous length, but without that little bitter core which lies hidden in *Tristram Shandy*. Ideas are often adopted for the sake of their paradoxes and discarded as soon as they cease to startle. He gives his audiences a sense of intellectual activity – but they often imagine they have exercised their brains when they have really done no more than strain their eyes at the startling convolutions of a tumbler.

Barrie was as ill at ease in the world as Shaw is confident. Favoured from the very start of his career by Fortune he remained a misfit. He invented a dream world of sexless wives who mothered and understood their husbands, of children who never grew up because they had never really been born. His plays were cloyingly sweet, but there had been no dramatic writer since the seventeenth century who knew his business so well. The opening act of *Dear Brutus* for example could not be bettered: from the opening line as the ladies drift in after dinner he holds you with his Ancient Mariner's eye. He wrote with ease and grace and he was a consummate craftsman: 'Had you with these the same but brought a mind.' But yet when all is said, he *had* enlarged the subject matter of our drama: he had improved its prose style: yet it is odd that his plays should have led nowhere.

One great dramatist was working in our century: one pictures him reading Flaubert in Paris, walking the boulevards to keep warm and save coal, learning the kind of seriousness which the French can teach better than any other nation: the intense seriousness of finding the right word and the right method whether you are writing farce or tragedy. This is the seriousness you do not find in Shaw or Barrie or Galsworthy – from whom pity for an unrealized lower-class drove out every consideration of style or form. But Synge exchanging the boulevards for the West Coast of

Ireland, lying flat on the bedroom floor of his inn with his ear to a crack, recording the phrases of the peasantry with scrupulous accuracy, was as careful and serious an artist as Flaubert. He reminds one of 'the chief inquisitor' in Browning's poem:

> He took such cognisance of men and things,
> If any beat a horse you felt he saw;
> If any cursed a woman he took note;
> Yet stared at nobody—they stared at him.

The Shadow in the Glen, The Riders to the Sea: these were the exquisite marginal drawings for the two great compositions, *The Well of the Saints* and *The Playboy of the Western World*. The last play caused a riot in the Dublin theatre where it was first presented – but no riot was ever caused in London. The excessive tolerance of that city (often amounting to indifference) allows it to accept everything without protest. Indifference can almost have the air of charity; but you cannot live on indifference, and Synge had not the secret of his fellow Irishman to shake London audiences into attention – he would not have wanted the secret. His work was done for the work's sake; personality was something to be excluded at all costs. The only hostility he aroused was in such places as the *Punch* office: a few comic writers wrote sneering little parodies of the Irish manner as they had written little sneering parodies of the Russian manner. Parodies sometimes have effects their authors never dreamed of, and I remember that my own first introduction to Synge was a parody in *Punch* when I was about fourteen years old – I went about for days with the magic of the silly jest in my ears.

Synge died young and again there was no successor; even in Ireland every new playwright had to begin over again and conquer the enmity of the Irish people.

In this short survey we have reached our own times, and it is a little invidious to hand out bouquets and poisoned chalices to contemporaries. But it is impossible not to notice the dead end. There are fine plays, but no single figure dominates and directs his age as Dryden and Jonson did. One cannot say the poetic drama shows no sign of life, when one has seen the success of *Murder in the Cathedral*. Somerset Maugham in *Our Betters* wrote perhaps the best social comedy of the century, and in *The Sacred Flame* he certainly wrote one of the worst dramas. Ronald Mackenzie in *Musical*

A caricature by Grace Plunkett of a performance of Synge's comedy The Playboy of the Western World, *which caused a riot at its first performance in Dublin in 1907. The audience was outraged by the plot – Irish peasants shelter and even adore a self-confessed murderer. Synge fell in love with Molly Allgood who played Pegeen Mike and she inspired his last play,* Deirdre of the Sorrows, *performed in 1910, after Synge's early death.*

Chairs made a magnificent beginning under Tchekhov's influence and was then killed in a motor accident. J. B. Priestley has tried to enlarge the contemporary subject matter with the help of Dunne, and you cannot say experiment is quite dead so long as Sean O'Casey and Denis Johnstone are writing. As for craftsmanship, Noël Coward has all his contemporaries beaten. He is the best craftsman since Barrie and unlike Barrie is able to disguise his sentimentality, coming into the open only occasionally in such pieces as *Cavalcade*. Only as the years pass and the contemporary idiom changes does his sentimentality begin to show, emerging as the dye washes off, like the colour of a stolen horse. One other dramatist I should like to include here, and that is Vernon Sylvaine, the author of *Women Aren't Angels* and other farces designed for the Robertson Hare, Alfred Drayton

Noël Coward as Elyot Chase and Gertrude Lawrence as Amanda Prynne preparing to elope together in Coward's comedy Private Lives *(1930). Elyot and Amanda were previously married to each other; now divorced they have re-married and find they have adjoining hotel rooms on their honeymoons. The play provided the young Laurence Olivier, who played Victor Prynne, with one of his earliest successes.*

combination. These plays with their great technical skill and their very national humour – full of discarded trousers and men dressed up in their wives' clothes and jealous women and timid husbands – are much more serious in the aesthetic sense than such fake tragedies as *The Sacred Flame* and *Loyalties*, which are exclusively written for the stalls and the upper circle.

It is a 'bitty' picture, the contemporary theatre – so many talented authors, so many plays of great competence and even of some seriousness, and yet surrounding every effort this sense of a huge public indifference. In that lies the chief distinction between the English and the American theatre: over here we write perhaps just as many good plays, but in New York they have a good audience. There is in the air an interest, an excitement – at any moment, you feel, the great dramatist may appear again because the audience is ready to receive him.

The economics of the London theatre have a great deal to do with this indifference: the huge theatre rents make managers unwilling to take risks, and like cinema companies they stick to the familiar pattern of entertainment (it is the small theatres – the Westminster, the Mercury, the Duchess and the Unity – which have been responsible for most of the experiments we have seen of late years). The rents, too, raise the price of seats, so that theatre-going becomes the privilege of an economic class and of middle age. The young and the poor may squeeze into the gallery, but the 'Gods' are powerless to influence the entertainment far below them.

But the picture is not wholly dark: the 'Old Vic' has kept Shakespeare before the people, the small theatres are there, and it is unlikely that the high rental of the West End will survive the war. The indifference of London to living art has been the indifference of a class, of the well-to-do and the professional man cut to pattern by his education. The theatre is bound up with the world's fate as it has always been: young, lyrical, conceited in the first Elizabethan theatre: dark with disillusionment and violence in the Jacobean; clever and conscienceless and making hay while the sun shone in the interval between two revolutions; moribund, living on the imagination of the past during the age of reason; journalistic and humanitarian during the reign of Victoria; confused and indecisive in our own times. . . . Now we are heading either for chaos of such long duration that the theatre will not survive our civilization, or a world so new and changed it may well be that in the theatre it will seem as though Elizabeth were on the throne again.

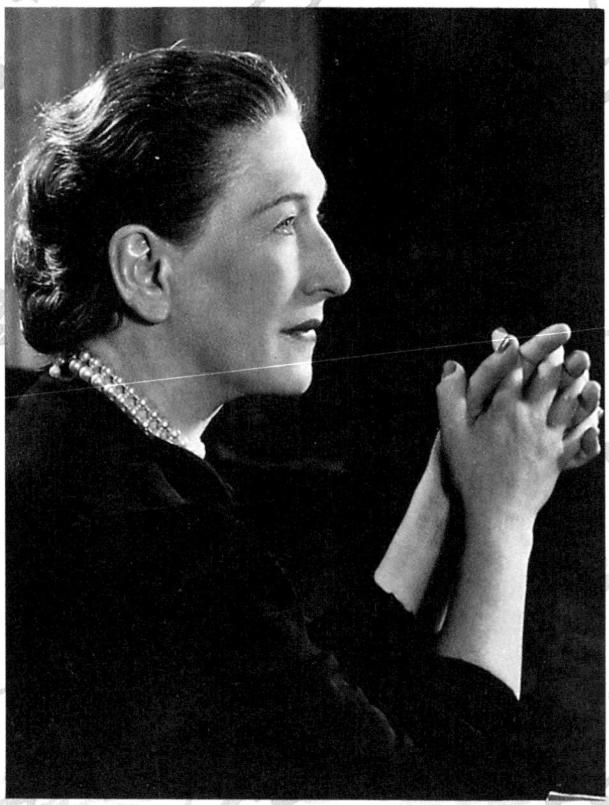

Novelists

ELIZABETH BOWEN

THE English novel, from its beginning on, has been the subject of so much critical writing that one may feel there remains little to add. Its characteristics have been defined; its development has been noted; influences upon it have been traced. In so far as all this may enlarge our pleasure in reading, we owe thanks to the critic. I do, however, see one danger – that too much information about great novels may make us less spontaneous in our approach to them – though they offer entrancing subjects for study, they were in the first place written to be enjoyed. It would be sad to regard as lecture-room subjects books that were meant to be part of life. As things are, are our classical English novels not often left to the honour of our high-up shelves, where they receive little other attention than the periodic dusting of their tops, while that place for which their lively authors designed them, the place on the book-table by the arm-chair, is taken by modern writers whose chief attraction is that we have not yet been required to find them 'good'?

We lose much if we ignore, or honour in name only, so living a part of the English heritage. And now, when the English spirit stands at its full height, to do so would be a double loss. England's past in art, as well as in history, has helped to build up her heroic To-day. It is natural to want our writers beside us as we face this new phase of human experience. And painters and writers, however long dead, however far back their place in actual time, remain, in their living art, our contemporaries. Their domain is always the domain of living men; it is to us, the living, that they are speaking now. This is as true of the novelists as it is of the painters or poets – as true, but not so easily recognized. Why? Because while in painter or poet we expect the sublime (or timeless), in the novelist we expect the familiar, the day-to-day. The novel, we feel, should keep close to life. Whatever seems unlikely is fatal to it. The novelist must be a man of his own day – and, as that day of his gives place to another, and as that other gives place to our own, may we not feel that he depicts only what was, so

Elizabeth Bowen, photographed in the early 1950s.

that his judgments seem to lose their point; How, the would-be reader may ask, can I find the familiar, the convincing, the likely, in a novel written two hundred years ago?

The answer, of course, is that while novelists must belong to their own day, the great novelist is not confined by that. Poor novels do pass away with their time; they pass because they concerned themselves only with the ephemeral parts of human experience, not with its lasting essentials. But in the great novel, we recognize those essentials that run through all experience, independent of time. We may, in fact, see for the first time what those essentials are. We see, too, why fundamentally men and women have changed so little. In a novel that has been great enough to survive the years, we shall find very little that is unfamiliar or queer. Any feeling of queerness evaporates in the course of the first pages. Differences of speech, costume, habits, manners do not affect us as we had thought they would: instead, we are made aware of the underlying likeness of life then to life as it is to-day.

The English novel, the novel proper, began in the Age of Reason – in fact, at a time when people thought for themselves – and reason has continued to be its godmother. But the genius that gave the novel its truth and life is, at the same time, something beyond the scope of reason; a sort of romantic miracle. In the course of the English novel, since its beginning, the English have continued to show and to see themselves – islanders, haughty, puzzled, at once saved and graced by a comicality to which they are not blind. The novel has been an overflow of a number of English people's feeling for their own life – and, also, it voices a criticism. It is as givers of one particular sort of pleasure, and inspirers of a particular sort of interest, that I shall discuss the English novelists. While I shall hope to be fair, I cannot avoid the influence of my own taste. I read for pleasure, and it must be remembered that I write as a pleasure-seeker and not a judge.

Of the English novel, before the eighteenth century, there were several curious false dawns. These attempts at the novel have a sort of interest for their own sakes. In the England of Queen Elizabeth the demand for entertainment was general, and the arts made a noble response to it. English drama then came, as we know, to its greatest height – and, as the mass of the people could still not read, drama continued to be the popular art. Writers who wrote anything other than plays addressed themselves to a literate, elegant upper class, and Elizabethans who did experiment in the novel either shared or flattered the Court's taste. The way was prepared for story-tellers by an existing vogue for Italian tales – this not the first nor the last of invasions of foreign fancy that have reached the English shore. First by late Renaissance Italy then by France, the English have been at once englamoured and shocked. By the time John Lyly, a Kentish man born in 1553, brought out his *Euphues*, translations from the Italian had set up a pretty high standard in artifice. Of this Lyly was so careful not to fall short that he decidedly over-reached himself; also, he gave his first story a foreign scene. In *Euphues, the Anatomy of Wit*, published in 1579 and followed a year later by *Euphues and his England*, all late Renaissance influences appear. There are great flights of discourse; everything is kept at the highest possible level above the everyday. The hero Euphues, his romantic friend Philautus and the lady who proves false to them both, leave few subjects of gallant or philosophic interest untouched. In the second half of the story the high-minded Euphues visits England, and comments on much that he finds there. *Euphues* had an immediate, hectic success in circles for which it was designed. But the success was brief – against Lyly's wrought-up style, with its hollow elegances, strained ingenuities, and overload of classical references there came a revulsion that was severe. Common sense began to assert itself, and enthusiasts felt that they had been fooled. Ridicule swept away *Euphues* – which is now chiefly remembered as having added a word to the English vocabulary. . . . The *Arcadia* of Sir Philip Sidney (born at Penshurst, 1554) fared a good deal better, as it deserved. The *Arcadia* is a sort of sustained dream, and also it has the consistency of a book written to please oneself – for Sir Philip, by himself for some time at his sister's house in the country, undertook the *Arcadia* for this reason alone. Courtier-soldier, traveller, lover, poet and man of the world, Sir Philip brought to his narrative prose-poem unusual feeling and innate stylishness. In the *Arcadia*, pairs of lovers wander in the seclusion of a pastoral world – though on this is imposed a complex plot. When, in 1590, four years after its author's death in battle, the *Arcadia* appeared (against his wishes, for he had asked that it should be burned), it went straight to the hearts of the *beau monde*, to whom, in the heated pressure of Court life, pastoral distances seemed idyllic – in fact, the theme of Arden was here. Though Sidney's lovers show less spirit than Shakespeare's, the breeze from *Arcadia* continued to blow sweet; and, not in itself deeply original, for pastorals had already been done abroad, the book was to be in its turn followed by a number of imitations in this genre.

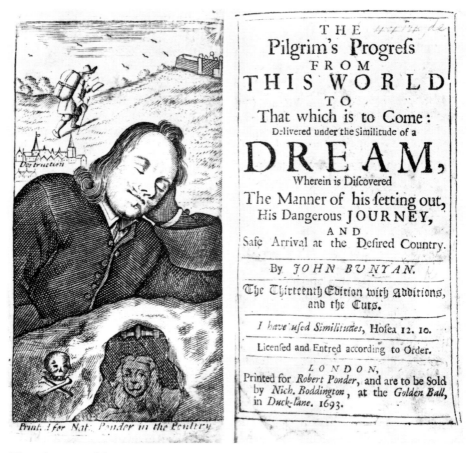

The title-page and frontispiece to The Pilgrim's Progress. *Bunyan's powerfully simple prose and narrative force had a great influence on the development of English fiction.*

John Greene (born in Norwich about 1560) belongs with the rakes and the realists. When he left Cambridge for London it was not to come to Court but to pick up a living by pamphleteering and the writing of plays. His trade was tough, his companions low. In this milieu, a gust of contempt for the unreal made him discard the *Euphues* influence under which his own first story, *Mamillia*, had been penned at Cambridge in 1583. So his succeeding stories, though still romantic, have that progressive strength that comes from a truer view. But more important were his pamphlets, that, in story-interest and length, began to approach short novels; in these he broke away from the courtly idea and wrote of the stinking, stewing London he knew – whether fine nostrils liked it or not. In this break with flattery and illusion, Greene came to be followed by 'ingenuous, ingenious, fluent, facetious Thomas Nash' (born at Lowestoft, 1567), who also developed the satiric attacking style.

So the Elizabethan period closes with two very opposite tendencies in the air. And a place for the narrative that was to become the novel had been at least made – though now that place was to stay empty for some time. With the end of Elizabeth's reign some creative urge subsided, and experiments came to a standstill.

In the seventeenth century, in which so much happened, little worth speaking of happened to the novel. John Bunyan was, it is true, to give, with his *Pilgrim's Progress* (1678), one of our grandest examples of story-telling. But first, the theatre kept its hold over the people – though drama was in a state of noisy decline; then, battles and metaphysics came with the Civil War. In 1642 the Puritan parliament closed the theatres, and, to escape from an oversevere world, pleasure-loving society turned to reading, and sought again – this time as an anodyne – the seductions of the imported romance. France now supplied the demand. Long-winded reconstructions of chivalry helped the ladies and gentlemen of the defeated faction through the Commonwealth gloom, and when the Restoration brought out the sun again the French romances could more freely circulate. For the English, the Frenchmen could hardly write fast enough – and quite soon English imitators sprang up. One cannot praise, and need not discuss, the results. However, with regard to the novel, the century had not a quite barren close: in 1692 one exquisite tale, *Incognita*, came from Congreve the dramatist. But the theatre was entirely to claim Congreve – it was having another tremendous boom. Literature, apart from dramatic art, was to be the domain of a few exquisite but rather detached minds. Vigorous invention and curiosity went, rather, to scientific research.

Story-telling, however, had one more likely recruit in the person of Mrs Aphra Behn. Though there were unkind judgments of this lady, she had one great merit: she wrote from experience. She had lived abroad, and she had lived to the full. Though subject to flights and foolishness, she had energy – more energy, some people considered, than was becoming in her sex. There was a tendency, due to last a long time, to regard professional novel-writing as an immodest, too dashing occupation for women; in fact, well on into the nineteenth century gentlewomen whose novels found publication remained anonymous, or used pen-names.

Mrs Aphra Behn, whose fiction combines realism with lurid romance, often (like Defoe) presented her work as a factual record: her Memoirs, *once accepted as genuine autobiography, are now thought to be largely invented.*

When, in 1698, Mrs Behn's two best-known novels, *Oroonoko* and *The Fair Jilt*, appeared, she had already been dead some years. *Oroonoko*, with its negro hero, put out that idea of the noble savage that Rousseau was to make popular with a romantic age. Aphra Behn is at least a landmark: the rest of the sub-heroic nonsense of her period vanished, leaving behind for the novel only a bad name.

The seventeenth century, all the same, produced the England that was to produce the novel. Out of the Civil War a new kind of English self-consciousness had been born. Social thought was already upon its way. The new interest in science had made people objective, curious, analytical. The complexity of the spirit of man was recognized – and, with this, his tie to the natural world. Most important, a new class had come into conscious power – the middle class, self-reliant, anti-feudal and sturdy. This class was to ask from art something new. The courtly idea had gone for ever to be succeeded by the democratic idea.

Disabused, critical, liking fact and inclined to rate fancy low, why should the eighteenth century have give birth to the novel? For some time, indeed, the brilliant essayists reigned. But it was two of these, Steele and Addison, who by their sketches in the *Tatler* (1709–11) and the *Spectator* (1711–12) made a step forward towards the novel by creating interest in character – or, should one say, heightening interest that had begun to exist? The members of Mr Bickerstaff's Club (in the *Tatler*) and Sir Roger de Coverley and his friends (in the *Spectator*) stepped from print into life with an utter convincingness. These were individual people; no longer the dreary 'types' who had dominated the English story and play. Only continuous narrative of their actions was needed to make Sir Roger and the others into characters in a novel – but this their creators did not choose to supply.

Daniel Defoe (a butcher's son born in London in 1660) perceived character, though he put action first: though what straighter approach to character could there be than the story of a man alone with himself? – and

The frontispiece to Defoe's Robinson Crusoe *(1719); the plot for this early masterpiece of the novel is based on the adventures of a Scottish sailor, Alexander Selkirk, whom Defoe had met.*

Robinson Crusoe, Defoe's first great work of fiction, was published in 1719. Defoe started late in fiction but not in writing: pamphlets, verses, satires, treatises had for years poured from his ready pen. Disgrace, a stand in the pillory and the loss of his business (he had started a brick kiln at Tilbury) had, by following on his double-edged pamphlet, *The Shortest Way with the Dissenters* (1702), already shown him his pen's danger – and power. He paid high for a laugh that no one else had enjoyed. When Defoe returned to his craft it was in a desperate spirit; starvation faced him and his family. By this time, however, he had the public taped; he resolved to make profit out of its gullibility, and the possibilities of fiction, to this end, at once presented themselves to him. He wrote up the case of a Mrs Veal who after her death appeared to a friend in Canterbury, and he did not fail to put Mrs Veal across. Defoe developed two great assets: plausibility and a superb style, at once matter-of-fact and evocative. His English has, to my mind, never been bettered: it is the ideal narrator's prose. After *Robinson Crusoe* came, in 1721, *Moll Flanders* – a great fascinating acute short book on no account to be missed by anybody. The bad beauty who names it is immortal: never was a life lived with more style. *Colonel Jack* came in 1722, and *Roxana* in 1724.

Everything that Defoe wrote reads as true. (He carried this so far as to be able to fake memory in his *Journal of the Plague Year*.) He sets up for us the important rule that a story-teller must be believed. It is true that he tested his plausibility on no subject so fantastic as that of the *Gulliver's Travels* (to give the book its short name) of Dean Swift – published in 1726. Swift's vast satiric imagination did not disdain, in *Gulliver's Travels*, the minutest details that would convince. Though the head may say to the reader, You know, this could not have happened, the imagination answers, It surely did. We see – and so we believe. In fact, to Defoe and Swift the English novel owes its powerful start. We have come to the end of the false dawns. The novel could only come into power when it took account of the forces of common sense.

Two elements of the novel were, thus, waiting – likely and living character, likely and living plot. But a third was needed, to merge these two. What was this? – interest in human relationships. The tract in which men and men, or men or women, affect, act on and conflict with each other was still waiting to be explored. It had been accepted that it is from a man's character that his actions spring. One had now to see the effect that one man or woman, by acting in character, had on the action or character of another. It had, too, to be seen that human behaviour seldom follows a set course (or course planned in the head), being often deflected by accidents. The nature and cause of the accidents that deflect behaviour might be called the stuff of the novel. Most often, these are psychological: conflicting desires between two people are more important than a tempest or a coach being overturned. One can see why the novel must have love interest – though in as wide a sense as you like.

And the novelist had to accept a fact known to his readers – that behaviour, however wide it zigzags, very seldom goes over certain set bounds. What sets these bounds? Society, what one might call the world of the everyone-else, that world in which each man or woman, by being born, takes up his or her inherited place. The relation of a man to society is an integral part of the concept of any novel. In the eighteenth century, the idea of society crystallized: the novel, in fact, was the product of a great social age. A man's relationship to society was seen as his first important and human one – he might fly from or defy society by becoming a hermit or vagabond, but he could not ignore it, for its existence gave him his meaning and shape. It was seen, I think rightly, that the fact that human beings do not live for themselves only, in vacuo, makes them more rather than less interesting.

This new contemplative interest in human beings was not on the level of poetry: sublimity played little part in it. The medium for its expression was prose narrative – but this would have to contain much. England being now ripe for the novel, the novel came. The public sprang to meet *Pamela*, published in 1740.

Samuel Richardson, the middle-aged London printer who became the author of *Pamela*, was a pursy, not interesting little man. Born in 1689, son of a joiner in Derbyshire, he had received a limited education, had come to London as an apprentice, done well and married his master's daughter. His experience of the world was limited – as some absurdities in *Pamela* show.

His life was troubled more by domestic griefs – there were many deaths in his family – than by emotional storms. His personal tameness makes all the odder his faculty – one is entitled to call it genius – for the analysis of the human heart. He is said, as a prim cold-blooded little boy of thirteen, to have been the confidant of a group of young ladies for whom he indited love-letters; and this precocious knowledge of love, at an age before one feels love, may account for much. Certainly, given the masculine temperament of the eighteenth century, Richardson's knowledge of

Pamela is married: *one of a series of paintings by Joseph Highmore illustrating Richardson's Pamela. Mr B.'s marriage to his mother's chambermaid was seen by some eighteenth-century readers as the triumph of a scheming minx and by others as the rightful reward for a persecuted and suffering woman, intimately and sympathetically portrayed by the novelist.*

women is extraordinary. His detractors might say that he spied on women rather than felt for them – certainly Richardson's heroines arouse (as he intended) solicitude rather than desire. (Fielding's heroines, on the other hand, are desirable before everything.) In *Pamela*, marred, as I say, by absurdities and more than a little shocking in its success philosophy, Richardson no more than foreshadows his coming powers. The *réclame* that *Pamela* gained him, the many new doors that opened to the successful author, he was artist enough to put to a good use. Also he learned a lesson from the experience of having *Pamela* ridiculed – of Fielding's ruthlessness I have yet to speak. In the eight years between *Pamela* and *Clarissa,* Richardson came out of his chrysalis. *Pamela* is a slight story brilliantly told. Of *Clarissa,* at the end of two hundred years, we may say: this remains one of the finest novels we have.

But *Pamela* is more than an innovation. To what can we trace the charm of this shocking book? Partly to the unerringness with which the sense of predicament is sustained. Partly to the vivacity of the dialogue. Partly to the intimacy of the manner – the book is written in letters, but it is more than that. Richardson not only adored detail but had an unfailing sense of its place in art.

Those who do not like him find his atmosphere too indoor – claustrophobic, in fact. It is true that his characters are constricted by their emotions into a tiny, oppressive world. . . . Pamela Andrews, little waiting-maid of fifteen, adorably pretty, a chaste minx, is left, by the death of her mistress and patroness, exposed to the evil designs of that lady's son, Mr B. From the slender defences she clings to at his Bedfordshire country house, Mr B. whisks Pamela off to his still more lonely estate in Lincolnshire.

'About eight o'clock at night' (Pamela writes to her parents, for whose peace of mind she seems to have no regard) 'we entered the courtyard of this handsome, large, old and lonely mansion, that looks made for solitude and mischief, as I thought by its appearance, with all its brown nodding horrors of lofty elms and pines about it. Here, I said to myself, I fear is to be the scene of my ruin. . . .'

Crude is hardly the word for Mr B.'s goings-on. And he is not even high-spirited. There comes the crucial occasion when Pamela's virtue is only saved by her collapse into alarming fits. Mr B., unnerved, thinks again: he ends by proposing marriage. Whereupon, Pamela, idealist in behaviour, accepts the husband she has up to now considered a mean, inestimable young man. The book's morality founders on this rock, and Pamela's bridal prosperity, though described with spirit, leaves one cold. The book, with unconscious cynicism, is sub-titled *Virtue Rewarded.*

One stands dumb, all the same, before the accomplishment of this first English novel. So did the world of its day. But the moral flaw in the book was perceived, without mercy, by at least one mind. It was on *Pamela's* weakness that Fielding pounced. Henry Fielding, Richardson's junior by nine years, had been born to many advantages that the printer, through no fault of his own, lacked. Fielding was a gentleman, a wit, a rake and a scholar. Born at his grandfather's country house near Glastonbury in 1707, educated at Eton, he found himself with remarkably little money and had been by turns journalist, playwright, barrister. By the time he read *Pamela* he was tough, poised, satiric – but something more. The full possibilities of this new form, the novel, may or may not at first have appeared to him. We know that he set out on his *Joseph Andrews* in a spirit of pure burlesque.

In *Joseph Andrews*, published 1742, Fielding gives Richardson's Pamela Andrews a brother Joseph, virtuous as herself and exposed to equal difficulties. The handsome young footman too well pleases his widowed employer's eye. His employer is Lady Booby, the aunt by marriage of Richardson's sinister Mr B. Mr B. – it could not have been more annoying – is thus made to enter Fielding's pages as young Mr Booby, with Pamela as his exceedingly snobbish bride. Richardson called *Joseph Andrews* 'a lewd and ungenerous engrafture' – and probably did not stop at that. But neither did Fielding stop at his burlesque – the novel ran far away from it, to our eternal gain. Joseph may be the hero, but he is soon eclipsed by the outsize figure of Parson Adams – Joseph's friend and patron, with his big heart, big family and big fist, his erudition and innocence, his Christian humility and his hot temper, his astounding get-up, optimism and constantly mislaid and forgotten horse. When Joseph flies from Lady Booby's in London, he meets Parson Adams, who is looking for him. Fanny, Joseph's young village love, has also left home to seek him – so these three range the country together on a much-interrupted journey home. And what country they travel, and in how roaring a spirit! If solicitude is the note of Richardson's novels, zest is the note of Fielding's. Strongly under the influence of Cervantes, he loved movement, the fantastic, the outdoor. In this first book we feel the author getting into his stride. Fielding had more to carry than Richardson, and so the content of every one of his novels is always a little more than their form will hold. But his very prodigality is superb. He is the masculine writer par excellence; in no other Englishman who has written has the masculine quality been so pure. Among the other sex one might say that only Jane Austen has been his counterpart – she wrought her own femininity into an art as tempered and as dispassionate.

On Richardson, the umbrage occasioned by *Joseph Andrews* had been having a far from bad effect, for in 1748 he published *Clarissa* – which one might call the corrective to *Pamela*. Here is the same situation, but with another approach – and from it breathes the real horror *Pamela* lacks. In

Henry Fielding: an etching after Hogarth. The novels are accompanied by a volume of statutes and the sword and scales of Justice, alluding to Fielding's work as a magistrate.

her bitter struggle with Lovelace, Clarissa Harlowe has – unlike Pamela in her struggle with Mr B. – nothing to gain. She is a young beauty, born to her own position, till lately adored by her proud family, and asking no more than to go on being tranquilly happy in her country home, Harlowe Place. In fact, she asks no more than to keep herself – but this is what Lovelace hates her to do. Threatened at home by an odious marriage, Clarissa is tricked into flight with Lovelace, who has continued to offer her a protection that should be completely disinterested. No sooner is she upon the road with him than he justifies her instinctive mistrust, and by a series of outrages breaks down – here is the core of the tragedy – the love for him she had been so ready to feel. In his hatred of what he calls her pride – though this hatred is knit up with a desperate love – he makes her suffer every abuse of the power from which she is unable to free herself. Clarissa, in the end, dies, but dies with her colours flying: though Lovelace, having drugged her, has once stolen her body, they both know that her spirit remains intact. Steadily, she has refused the marriage he offers: she cannot marry without love, cannot love without honour, and cannot honour the man who, by every action, has ruined his (not her own) honour in her eyes. One may say that, in this stand she took up, Clarissa was not only high above Pamela but very much in advance of her own time – in which (with a cynicism that was to last) marriage was supposed 'to make everything all right'. Clarissa may well have been found exacting. Was she, perhaps, proud? Her sense of her own pathos does a little alienate us from her – 'A young creature like I am', she often says.

The story is (like *Pamela*) told in letters: Clarissa and Lovelace each have confidants of their own sex. But the letters read more like journals: there are pages and pages of brilliant dialogue. Also, a circle of other characters is made to surround the hating lovers – most notable is the figure of Anna Howe, Clarissa's high-spirited, gallant girl friend, who has Mr Hickman for quiet *fiancé*. But the outstanding figure of the book is not Clarissa; it is Lovelace himself – the brilliant neurotic rake. The pathological complexities of Lovelace, the extravagance of his reactions are, I say firmly, absolutely convincing; I say this firmly because, by some critics, Lovelace has been denounced as 'impossible'.

Clarissa has a compactness (in spite of its great length) and a saturation in its own moral atmosphere to which few novels have so completely attained. It has a convincingness nothing can break through. . . . In 1753 Richardson followed up with *Sir Charles Grandison*, the tale of a model baronet and his ladies, but after *Clarissa* this lacks emotional power and seems diffuse, artificial and slow. France as well as England wept over *Clarissa* – but France was shocked by Fielding's ultra-English *Tom Jones*. It is interesting to compare Fielding's masterpiece – published in 1749, one year after *Clarissa* – with Richardson's. Fielding's conscience – or call it morality – was a thing tempered out of his own furious living; Richardson's conscience remained a theory – though a theory brought to a fine point. The predicament of the conscience is the real preoccupation of *Tom Jones*, in spite of the novel's lordly, spacious, picaresque overlay and its rough-house scenes. Tom Jones, the handsome foundling, is a bad lad who constantly disappoints the squire who brought him up and deviates from his ideal love for Sophia. Circumstances combine to treat Tom hardly, and he hardily does what he can with them. Turned out by the squire, he rides the country with his self-seeking Sancho, Partridge, and, coming to London to seek Sophia, is more than half embroiled by all the wiles of the town. In Sophia Western, who 'with all the gentleness which a woman can have, had all the spirit which she ought to have', Fielding creates the first of the English novel's adorable heroines. The book is, again, pre-eminent in its comedy characters: to have sat through *Hamlet* with Partridge, as Tom did, can have been only second in pleasure to sitting through *Hamlet* with Miss Bates. And there is Squire Western, baited in argument by his sister, that blue-stocking and snob, till 'Damn Milton!' roars the suffering Squire. Squire Western remains the prototype of one very marked kind of landed English commoner. 'I hate all lords,' he says simply, 'they are a parcel of courtiers and Hanoverians , and I will have nothing to do with them.' That is that. The other type – more thoughtful but as feudal – is represented by Squire Allworthy. 'Love,' says Squire Allworthy, to the (apparently) erring Jenny Jones, 'however much we may corrupt and pervert its meaning . . . remains a rational passion.'

This idea – or ideal – of the rational passion is strong in Fielding, as it is in his race, as it was in his century. It had even been, in a sense, to this ideal that Richardson's bewildered Clarissa clung. And the idea of love on this plane has continued to rule the English novel – one may say that, to an extent, it has limited it. The French and the Russians have been left to explore love's inherent principles of disorder and pain.

Fielding's *Amelia* followed *Tom Jones* in 1751. While Fielding wrote this last novel he had been at once an ailing and, as a Westminster magistrate, a very busy man, and though the book shows no descent in feeling, it does show a certain decline in force. Amelia, the heroine, is a married woman, constantly tried but never disillusioned by the weaknesses of her husband, Captain Billy Bond. Her patience, with its triumphant saneness, on the whole suffers less than poor Billy's conscience – sporadic though that conscience may be.

I have given to Fielding and Richardson what may seem by the end of this book to be too much space. But surely they are important? Not only are they our two innovators, but it seems to me that, in their different work, all later English novels are present in embryo. These two represent two opposed, but equally real, aspects of the English temperament – in a sense, all succeeding English novelists descend from one or other of them. Also, these two men, by the time that their work was finished, had sent out like a challenge their sense of the novel's power, and had shown, without attempting to limit, what was likely to be the English novel's scope. I am sorry that, because of my use of space, I shall not be able to do anything like justice to Tobias Smollett, the Scotsman who, born in 1721, published his *Roderick Random* in 1748 – the same year as *Clarissa*.

Of Smollett, it may be said briefly that he perfected the picaresque romance – he had all the stuff for this, for, disappointed in his early hopes as a dramatist, he had, a navy doctor, gone to sea. After five years of adventure he returned to London, where he set up as a surgeon in Downing Street. *Roderick Random*, with its attractive hero and quick-moving scenes, obtained a success that justified him in trusting his fortune to his pen. Smollett was – as far as I know – the first novelist to attempt to define the novel. 'A novel', he says in one of his dedications, 'is a large diffused picture, comprehending the characters of life, disposed in different groups and exhibited in various attitudes, for the purposes of a uniform plan. . . . This plan', he adds, 'cannot be executed with propriety, probability, or success, without a principal personage to attract the attention, unite the incidents, unwind the clue of the labyrinth, and at last close the scene, by virtue of his own importance.' One criticism of Smollett is that his heroes fail to unite the incidents in the novels that they so often name – the incidents being too various for any one character to unite. He has, again, been accused of coarseness. In reality, the touchy, difficult Scotsman (few people knew him well) had a more delicate stomach than his contemporaries: the brutality that was the dark side of our Age of Reason inspired a sort of nausea in him – his reactions were the reactions of nausea. He excelled, perhaps overreached himself, in burlesque. . . . His *Peregrine Pickle* came in 1751, *Ferdinand, Count Fathom* in 1753, and his last and best novel, *Humphry Clinker*, with its postillion hero, in 1771. He admitted he owed much to foreign influences, to Cervantes and to Lesage's *Gil Blas*. His great lack, as an artist, was equanimity. And he bred, through no fault of his own, a most regrettable host of imitators, who threatened again to bring the name of the novel down.

The subtlety lacking in Smollett was brought to a fine point in Laurence Sterne. Born in 1713, at Clonmel in Ireland, son of a poor lieutenant, Sterne, upon leaving Cambridge, took holy orders. During his twenty years cure of a Yorkshire parish his cloth did not debar him from the enjoyment of privileged eccentricity: he fiddled, shot, had a circle of wild friends, wrote sermons, and all the time revolved a number of matters in the white heat of his curious intellect. The result was to be *Tristram Shandy*

– written in Yorkshire, published in London 1759. Contemporary London, dazzled, hardly knew what to think, and we hardly know how to speak now, of this unique book. *Tristram Shandy* bears no intellectual date. It is dementedly natural in its course, surrealist in its association of images. One does not attempt to 'follow' *Tristram Shandy*; one consigns oneself, dizzily, to it. This seems all the odder, because the plot – in so far as there is any plot – is static. The characters – Mr and Mrs Shandy, Uncle Toby, Corporal Tim, Yorick the parson, the dapper doctor – stand still, but soar and enlarge from their roots like trees. Young Tristram spends much of his time as an embryo: by the end of the book he is about five years old. The Widow Wadman's appearance is brief and fatal. One may say that, in the pages of *Tristram Shandy*, one finds the whole of English fantasy charted – and what a fantasy! This is a book that inspires volumes: one cannot do much with it in a paragraph. Some people hate Sterne: they say he is maddening and indecent. He is indecent: whether he is maddening depends on you. . . . In 1768 he published the *Sentimental Journey* – a fluid, delicious, capricious and on the whole 'easier' book.

Dr Johnson's *Rasselas*, not exactly a novel, left its impressive mark on the century. It was Johnson who, through an act of kind interference, brought to light the distracted Goldsmith's *Vicar of Wakefield*. Oliver Goldsmith, born in Ireland 1728, and educated at Trinity College, Dublin, had come grimly poor to London, after a series of Continental adventures, only to find a grimmer poverty there. The manuscript of *The Vicar of Wakefield* had moved about with his person, in and out of debtors' prisons, for some years: when the book did come to be published, in 1766, the author still maintained in his preface, 'There are an hundred faults in this thing.' He can but have felt, however, how his book's spirit transcends possible faults. With *The Vicar of Wakefield*, the eighteenth century's first note of intimate tenderness has been struck. Here is true virtue – humble and tried. The Primrose family, with their innocence, their hopes and fears, their lyrical domesticity, exist in an element that seems hardly literature, so unlike is this to the air of another book. Here are the beauty and pathos of youthfulness – the Vicar himself seems hardly old. And when poor lovely Olivia stoops to folly, never did such true sadness surround a fall. As to writing – Goldsmith is the most delicate narrative stylist the eighteenth century put out. He adds to Defoe's directness a poetic lucidity of his own. His comic sense has something rueful about it – all the same, he adds, with the figure of Mrs Primrose, to the English gallery of great silly women. Mrs Shandy was there before her; Mrs Bennet is to join her soon. With this gem, *The Vicar of Wakefield*, the first great age of the English novel closed.

But the age has a footnote, or epilogue, that one must not miss. Miss Fanny Burney, though only born, at King's Lynn, Norfolk, in 1752, by which year Fielding and Richardson had already finished their best work, comes in time to contribute the woman's view of the Age of Reason and its society. In view of the prejudice against lady writers, Miss Burney not only published anonymously but wrote in secrecy and with some sense of guilt. However, Dr Johnson's approval was later to justify her career. She was sheltered and nicely bred – the daughter of a doctor of music, whose move with his family up to London added interest to without ever disturbing the tenor of his domestic life – and when she wrote her two most successful novels she still knew little directly of the world. She, however, contemplates scenes of callousness that amount to brutality with just that equanimity Smollett lacked.

Fanny Burney lived to be Queen Charlotte's attendant at the secluded Court, to be chased round Kew Gardens by poor King George III in one of his fits of maniac playfulness, to record all this in a lively journal, and to marry and share the misfortunes of a French emigré, M. D'Arblay. Perhaps real life a little diminished her, for her early work is her best – as having the freshness of someone who still expects much from experience. This freshness endears to us her young heroines. She is not a great novelist – her men are flat figures, though expertly cut out, and her women lack what she lacked: intellect, passion, irony – but she is an engaging, ingenious, often convincing one. *Evelina*, her first novel, published 1778, is the story of *A Young Lady's Entrance into the World*, with the vicissitudes – largely aggressions by vulgar people – that attended it. Fanny Burney's heroines, unlike Jane Austen's, seldom rise above those social miseries that it is their creator's special joy to describe. Could Evelina, for instance, had she found herself in Clarissa Harlowe's position, have suffered more than she does in being seen about with the awful Branghtons? One doubts it. A subtle falseness of values impairs Fanny Burney's novels, for all their charm. In *Cecilia*, following *Evelina*, this weakness more plainly appears. Burney women, though they protest and blush, are made up of tacit acceptances. A *roué* could have seen Woman in these feminine novels and felt few stirrings of self-reproach; he could ask, 'Can one fundamentally wrong Woman, when she is not able to feel fundamental wrong?' The ardent spirit in woman had been already saluted by Fielding and Richardson: Jane Austen and the Brontës later made its voice heard.

We must take it that now, for a few decades, the first great English impulse towards the novel, the social impulse, seemed to come to a pause. Already a revolt against Reason, and against its controlling effects, seemed to be on its way. The escape from society, this time, was not to be to the green glades of Arcadia but to the haunted castle and beetling crag. Fancy, so long kept down, now violently reasserted itself. Horace Walpole's *The Castle of Otranto* (1764) was followed by a whole spate of horrific-fantastic tales, featuring demon lovers, shrieks, vaults. This gothic sub-literature is a specialist's subject: I have only room here to name two of its practitioners, Monk Lewis and Mrs Radcliffe – who closed the century with her *Mysteries of Udolpho* (1794). This crude opening of a romantic revival is, however, important, and must be noted: in it appears that shadowy, deep underneath of the English nature – a nature of which, in the great eighteenth-century novels, we have so far seen only the daylit, orderly top. (Though the dark has already come up through Richardson, with his 'brown nodding horrors of elms and pines'.) We shall observe how the nineteenth-century novelists attempted to keep in balance the English darkness and day. Apart from its gothic movement, the novel now tended to lapse and fall into disrepute. In quality it grew vapid; in quantity it was overproduced. Extravagant sensibility gave it its strongest colour; it was felt to threaten the not strong fortress of reason in a generation of Lydia Languishes.

Jane Austen seems to belong to no century. Her 'modernity' has been commented on – which is, I suppose, an agreeable way of saying that she is still some distance ahead of us. I have, earlier, coupled her name with Fielding's: she is like him in her feeling for comedy, her highness of spirit, and most of all, in so completely not being a muff. She was born in 1775, in Hampshire, at Steventon, of which her father was rector, and her earlier novels were written, though not published, within the bounds of the eighteenth century. Publication dates – *Sense and Sensibility*, 1811; *Pride and Prejudice*, 1813; *Mansfield Park*, 1814; *Emma*, 1816; *Persuasion* with *Northanger Abbey*, 1818 (after her death) – do not represent her novels' actual order in her working life. *Persuasion* was, in fact, her last novel, but *Northanger Abbey* – which owes its initial satiric idea to Mrs Radcliffe, as *Joseph Andrews* owed its to Richardson – had been written as far back as 1798, and *Pride and Prejudice*, under another title, was the first of her published novels to be written – in 1797, when she was twenty-two.

Herself a delighted reader of novels, Jane Austen saw no reason, and was to show no reason, why the novel should lapse from that place of honour that Fielding and Richardson gained for it. Her own and, I think, only explicit defence of the novel is to be come on early in *Northanger Abbey*, and here the spirit matches the irony. 'Yes, novels', she says, '. . . performances which have only genius, wit and taste to recommend them'. She took up her own pen, however, in no dogmatic spirit. She wrote, at her edge of the family parlour table, with just that zest for the scene and joy in discrimination with which she chose new ribbons, flirted and danced. But her genius was imperative. She surrounded each subject she took up with every feeling and faculty that she had. There has been a tendency to accept Jane Austen as no more than a faultless practitioner of the minute: her own remark (to a too fervent clergyman) about the two inches of ivory has been held against her. It is true that she made no effort to pass, through art, outside the range of her own, a gentlewoman's, experience: her novels depict the lives of leisured young men and women in country houses or on visits to Bath or London. Men (and women) in action were her subject, and with her vivid precision she placed action where, by the chance of her birth, she most often saw it – in drawing-rooms and ballrooms, on lawns, in shopping streets. But what she at once depicted and penetrated was not just *a* world, it was *the* world. She arrived at, and was able to fix for us, the denominators of desire, self-delusion and passion that are common to every kind of human experience. Her view of life, in fact, if confined to, was not confined by, drawing-rooms and lawns. She applies big truths to little scenes – so no scene stays 'little' under her hand. The constraints of polite behaviour serve only to store up her characters' energies; she dispels, except for the very stupid, the fallacy that life with the lid off – in thieves' kitchens, prisons, taverns and brothels – is necessarily more interesting than life with the lid on. It is true she has drawn no rebels: her people expect, and derive, pleasure from the straight-forward living of life. But they plan; they seek, with degrees of determination, ideal circumstances, ideal relationships inside that world they already know. They locate, and never far from themselves, possible darkness, chaos; they feel the constant threat of the wrong – be this only a mean act, a callous or a designing remark, a subtly deceiving proposition, a lie. The world Jane Austen creates remains an absolute world because of its trueness to its own scale.

Not only the charm but the strength of Jane Austen's novels resides in their being so innately grown-up. In enjoying the youthfulness of her

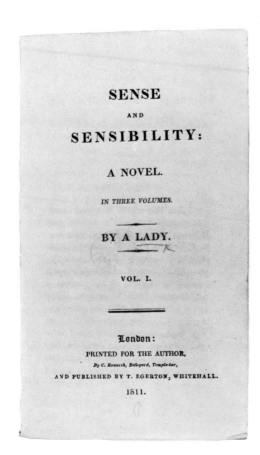

SENSE

AND

SENSIBILITY:

A NOVEL.

IN THREE VOLUMES.

BY A LADY.

VOL. I.

London:
PRINTED FOR THE AUTHOR,
By C. Roworth, Bell-yard, Temple-bar,
AND PUBLISHED BY T. EGERTON, WHITEHALL.

1811.

(above) *A pen and watercolour sketch of Jane Austen by her devoted sister Cassandra. Painted in about 1810, when the novelist was thirty-five, it is the only portrait of her to have survived.*

(left) *The title-page of Jane Austen's first published work,* Sense and Sensibility *(1811), which turns upon two sisters' contrasting attitudes to love and marriage – acceptance of the world as it is ('sense') and a romantic longing for the ideal ('sensibility').*

women – most youthful of all in their mistakes – we are at the same time conscious of something in them that remains ageless and poised. So high is this norm of maturity that infantilism, in one form or another, appears as the root of all faults and absurdities: it is imperfect grown-upness that makes people brag, fuss, prattle, play-act or flatter themselves. Among the heroines, poise appears most in her first, Elizabeth Bennet, and in her last, Anne Elliot. But also, Emma Woodhouse retains a lovable balance throughout her headstrong career, and deluded, naïve little Catherine Morland keeps not only Henry Tilney's but the reader's respect. Fanny Price and Elinor Dashwood remain just a shade too sober for many tastes. But one must see that Fanny's sobriety gives much to the structure of *Mansfield Park*, while Elinor acts as the counterpoise to unstable, brilliant Marianne. . . . Jane Austen has also been criticized for an imperfect evaluation of love: it is said that her leisurely, civilized young creatures

deny to the passion its true place. She was a great supporter of the rational passion, and the young men allowed to inspire this in her brilliant and her fastidious women are not – with the major exceptions of Mr Darcy and volatile Henry Tilney – men whom one feels would inspire much. Her tempting alternatives to reason – Willoughby, Frank Churchill, Henry Crawford – are always better done. But, as against this, with what gallant sparkling composure, almost Shakespearean, her heroines' flirtations are conducted, and with what fineness the early shades of attraction are recognized! Silence always falls on couples of plighted lovers – as though feeling paused outside a door. And, *Persuasion* – could there be a deeper picture of a woman loving too late, apparently without hope?

Technically – that is, as to matters of form, plot, characterization, dialogue, setting – Jane Austen remains the most nearly flawless of English novelists. She could not have been other than English – yet she stands a little apart from other writers we have in an artistry that no sentiment blurred, no theory narrowed and no rancour or prejudice side-tracked.

Born, north of the Border, four years before Jane Austen – in fact, in 1771 – Sir Walter Scott was to release England's imagination. Desire for exaltation, love of strangeness, had so far given birth only to gothic tales: Jane Austen had ridiculed mystery. Scott's majestic narrative poems – *The Lay of the Last Minstrel*, 1805; *Marmion*, 1808; *The Lady of the Lake*, 1810 – had first made England look North, and look North with awe. One was met by a landscape dark with clouds and feeling, charged with the past, lost battles, old memories and relentless dreams, a landscape against which the human figure could only stand out in heroic acts. England, who long ago with the Stuarts had accepted a line of Scottish kings, now began to drink in the Scottish tradition – a tradition that returned Fate to its place. (Eighteenth-century England, in common with most of rational Europe, had up to now stressed will rather than fate.) Scott, when he turned to the novel, showed the first great impulse that owed nothing to the sense of society – though it owed everything to the sense of race. What

Sir Walter Scott in the library at Abbotsford, the Scottish manor-house he created, reading the proclamation of Mary Queen of Scots previous to her marriage to Darnley. This painting of 1832 by William Allan hints at the literary and medieval world of Scott's imagination: the novelist is surrounded by part of his collection of antique armour; on the mantelpiece is a bust of Shakespeare.

Scott did for his own country in giving voice to its nature is Scotland's and not England's affair: what is certain is that he rushed in on England to fill an emotional vacuum. For the mannered, dry-witted age of the Regency, Jane Austen perfected the novel of manners but this same age received, as though it were parched, Scott's novels that rolled down on it like rain-clouds. And about the man himself there was something warm and commanding that seemed to mellow the air.

The first of his novels, *Waverley*, appeared in 1814 – the same year as *Mansfield Park*. *Guy Mannering* followed in 1815; *The Antiquary* shared 1816 with *Emma*. From then on, the Scott novels are too numerous and regular to enumerate; outstanding names and dates are: *The Heart of Midlothian* (1818), *The Bride of Lammermoor* (1891), *Ivanhoe* (1820), *Kenilworth* (1821), *Peveril of the Peak* (1822), *Quentin Durward* (1823), *Redgauntlet* (1824), *Woodstock* (1826), *The Fair Maid of Perth* (1828). *Count Robert of Paris* and *Castle Dangerous*, his last two short novels, appeared in 1832 – the year of his death.

The idea of the historical novel was in itself, to the England of that day, new. Novelty, linked with its own outstanding power, secured for *Waverley* immediate success. The past, with its accumulation of feeling, was presented with the likeliness of the present day. And when Scott dealt with his own day, as in *Guy Mannering* and *The Antiquary*, past-like emotion gave depth to the scene. He was less happy when, as a *tour de force*, he adventured – as in *Ivanhoe*, *The Talisman*, *Kenilworth* – into English history: reconstruction here is too obvious; the scenes seem to be cardboard, the people thin. He cut his art off, in fact, from its natural source when he detached himself from his own native mystery. He was truly creative only in regard to his own land. His people are epic figures or nothing, and he could see the epic only in people he instinctively knew. So his novels have their own psychic atmosphere.

Most of the plots contain some major heroic passion. The characters range from great to lowly – many are simple, wanderers, naïve narrative talkers, the trustful, the half-crazed. Scott's treatment of sexual love is stilted – less dishonest than shy. Love with him is always involved with some other aspect of fate. His style depends on emotion for force and lift; so that, when at times the emotion behind it lapses, one feels let down, and resents the verbosity. But such a style, with its poetic richness, was bound, coming when it did, to fecundate English prose. I am less concerned to claim Scott's Scottish novels for England than to show their effect on the English novelists.

The effect was, on the whole, a loosening one. As such, it was strongly resisted by William Makepeace Thackeray, who, son of a British official in India, had been born near Calcutta in 1811. Thackeray vowed himself to the anti-heroic. Consciously unfortunate Victorian, he was preyed upon by nostalgia for the eighteenth century – seldom does a nostalgia set in so soon. With him it was a case of 'Of thee I dream . . .'. Not only did he regret his own place in time, but he is said to have felt that he could have written better had he not been English: this seems strikingly true. Also, much happened to damp down in Thackeray anything like a spontaneous love of life – having received a gentleman's education, and formed along with that a gentleman's ample tastes, he lost his money and was condemned for some time to a seedy existence abroad: when he married, his wife became insane after four years. He lacked the resilience of Fielding, whom he so much admired; and in his attempts at realism he was infected, more than he may have realized, by the insincerities of his period.

Need to repair his fortunes in the first place drove Thackeray to the pen. He had been writing for papers for some years, under varying pseudonyms and with increasing success, when *Vanity Fair*, with his own name on the covers, began to appear in monthly parts in the year 1847–8 – all but a hundred years after *Tom Jones*. This first and great novel of Thackeray's creates for itself an epoch. It was an ambitious book that had not failed. Prodigal in incident, character, sense of period, saturated in humour, spontaneous in its criticism of life, it is in form, at the same time, absolutely controlled. Possibly Thackeray's natural bent was to write about wicked people rather than good. The *Vanity Fair* characters, stamped with life for ever, are headed by that great bad girl Becky Sharp, whose career across other lives her creator follows with a submerged laugh and, I think, some submerged love. The good – through their imperfect virtue – are fooled: Thackeray sees the vice in a sentiment. The length and variety of the book – there is everything in it from a good-bye to a girl's school to drama before the battle of Waterloo – are part of its merit: it suited Thackeray's powers to make a panoramic view of experience. He here uses perfectly his astringent style. The sub-title is *A Novel without a Hero* – and, in fact, there is no one central character, and nobody that one is enjoined to admire; he gave the book a moral rather than human plan. But this does not make it either abstract or cold. *Vanity Fair* is entrancing, engaging from first to last.

What happened to Thackeray after this? His powers, after *Vanity Fair*, seem to me to have horribly misdirected themselves. His conceptions remain spacious, his style sometimes masterly and always efficient. But I think he made a mistake in abandoning the complete moral detachment of *Vanity Fair*. In attempting to put across 'good' people, in attempting to make disillusionments a matter of tragedy rather than comedy, he commits himself to a sentimentality that is at once laboured and insincere. His anti-heroicism involves every character in the same tepid atmosphere. His *Esmond* (1852) is important as being the first *English* historical novel: the period of the story is Queen Anne. Thackeray, steeped in the Augustan Age, could now give his nostalgias rein: Steele, Swift, Addison walk and talk through the pages – but they seem to creak. In fact, throughout *Esmond* one gets the feeling that damp has got into the works.

Thackeray, drawn by Daniel Maclise in 1832, shortly before the loss of his inheritance drove him to journalism, caricature, and novel writing to earn a living.

The triangular situation between Esmond, Lady Castlewood and her daughter Beatrix is boldy conceived but timidly handled – Thackeray may have had this in mind when he implied that he would have liked to be French.

Pendennis (1848) had preceded *Esmond*; *The Newcomes* (1853–5) followed it. These two novels are interesting as documents of Thackeray's own class – the upper-middle – and age – the early Victorian. They contain some portraits of detestable women, fatally well drawn. *Pendennis, The Newcomes* are shells of great novels – or should one say great shells of novels? But life – and surely they once had life? – seems to have evaporated from them. Over good Colonel Newcome does anybody survive who could shed a tear? . . . No, the loose rich romantic fullness of Scott certainly did nothing to Thackeray.

As an acknowledged influence on Dickens, I do not remember having heard Scott named – but there must have been something propitious to Dickens's temperament in the atmosphere Scott had left behind. Dickens's subjects are as superficially prosaic as Scott's are evidently poetic, but romantic energy is common to both. Charles Dickens was born at Portsmouth in 1812 – a year after Thackeray. His father was a dockyard clerk whose character was to be idealized into Mr Micawber; his mother is said to have inspired Mrs Nickleby. Such an alliance was not likely to make for domestic stability: the family tottered along and now and then crossed the line that divides fecklessness from declared ruin. After a move to London there came a crash, and little Charles, as a debtor's visiting son, became familiar with the Marshalsea debtors' prison. To support himself, the boy of twelve worked in a blacking factory, filling and labelling pots. His father's release from prison set him free to attend a seedy school; he picked up enough learning to make himself into a solicitor's clerk. Later he taught himself shorthand, and, as reporter for several papers, sat in the gallery of the House of Commons. This was to be only one phase of his career as a journalist. He knocked about England, saw and tackled life, drew conclusions, collected fantastic facts. All his youth he had been an omnivorous reader; his feeling for 'story' had been developed young. So he wrung the most out of every experience: nothing that happened to Dickens went to waste. The class from which Dickens sprang – the English shabby-genteel, holding tight to the fringe of respectability – had been up to now ignored by art and society. It was the pathetic product of an age ruled by commercial ideas of success, in which human values were crude and on the whole mean. England was still unwilling to cope with

the bad conditions industrialism created. Can one wonder at Dickens's exaltation – call it sentimental – of the good heart? Can one wonder at his tenderness for the devices of fancy by which underdog people manage to live? The sociological aspect of Dickens I have not got room to discuss here. But remember that he had first been thrust into, and had later explored by his own will, abysses of injustice and human waste. Though success met him early – in fact, with the publication of the *Pickwick Papers*, in monthly parts, in 1836 – he never ceased to feel what he had seen. The buoyancy of his spirits did not make him a less implacable moralist. He brought up his picturesque, persuasive, sometimes extravagant art against the well-fed callousness that comes largely from lack of imagination – and he did live to see some reforms. He chose to appeal to feeling rather than thought – he *was* violently sentimental: leave it at that. But defiantly, perhaps involuntarily, what an artist he was! There is something superbly childish – I mean, unspoilt – about his imagination. He gives a child's value – a poor child's – to the enjoyment of sheer physical bliss – warm lit

(opposite) *Charles Dickens photographed in 1859 at the age of forty-seven, the year in which he published* A Tale Two Cities. (above) The Empty Chair: *this cartoon appeared in a London newspaper two weeks after Dickens's death in 1870. Based on a painting by Luke Fildes, it poignantly conveys the national sense of loss felt at the death of Britain's most popular novelist. Scenes and characters from Dickens's novels – including Oliver Twist asking for more, Mr Pickwick and Sam Weller, Mrs Squeers dosing the boys at Dotheboys Hall – celebrate the enduring nature of the creations of Dickens's imagination.*

rooms, trustworthy faces, the roar of a fire, the succulence of a chop. At the same time, he keeps a child's apprehensiveness of the weird, the unknown, the unsubstantially threatening. He gives loneliness, sense of loss or sense of betrayal all the frightful force they have for a child. Though he draws unconvincing or sugary pictures of 'straight' love, he is first-rate at depicting the sinister attachment – such as Rosa Dartle's to Steerforth – also, in the depiction of hero-worship. In fact, into all the love affairs in his books a queer adolescent strain of hero-worship, or idealization, enters on one or the other side. His linked senses of threat and of friendliness make him second to no other writer in penetrating the atmospheres of landscapes, houses and streets. And he is frightening in his sense of the power of all kinds of obsession and fantasy.

He was too much embroiled with his subject to be detached in his style. But his emotional vision sometimes produces the most mobile kind of English romantic prose. Read, for instance, the passage beginning 'The waters are out in Lincolnshire . . .' in Chapter II of *Bleak House. Bleak House* (1852–3) seems to me the most impressive, *David Copperfield* (1849–50) the most august and tender, and *Great Expectations* (1860–1) the most original of Dickens's novels. But no name of a novel of his is unknown, and few of his novels, I think, remain unread. In him the English genius finds a wide course: he is as comprehensive as any writer we have. His zest and humour have been likened to Fielding's. But he has in common with Richardson his perception of the nervous, or dusky, side of the human make-up.

When Dickens died, he left unfinished a mystery story, *Edwin Drood*. His growing preoccupation with mystery was due to his friendship with Wilkie Collins, who, born in 1824, was to do brilliantly in this genre. Wilkie Collins, in fact, may be called the grandfather of the English detective story. He had not only a great sense of human drama but a command, to be envied, of 'atmospheric' style – see the description of the tree-muffled Hampshire mansion at midnight, and of the dead lake, in *The Woman in White*. He also created – as in Count Fosco – superbly sinister figures, and drew some unforgettable scenes. His two greatest stories are *The Woman in White* (1860) and *The Moonstone* (1868).

Anthony Trollope, another friend of Dickens, has only lately come into his own again. Less intellectual and fastidious but also less arid than Thackeray, more stolid and less fantastic than Dickens, he seems to me the most sheerly able of the English Victorian novelists. He was honest enough about his own age to be able to give an objective picture of it; he

Anthony Trollope, photographed in 1864 by Julia Margaret Cameron, when he was completing his sequence of Barsetshire novels.

was less affected by pruderies than prepared to make discreet allowance for them. One cannot deny that, with the nineteenth century, a sort of fog did begin, in the English novel, to obscure some vital aspects of life. It became more difficult to write greatly because it became less possible to write truly. There was facetiousness on the subject of class, squeamishness on the subject of sex. One could no longer travel straight across country, as the eighteenth-century novelists had done. Evasions made for sentimentality. Anthony Trollope probably recognized that, for the Victorian novelist, absolute integrity was impossible; but he made towards an integrity of his own. . . . Born in 1815, three years after Dickens, he had an unhappy childhood (see his *Autobiography*): he seemed to himself to be born at a disadvantage – which makes one all the more admire the saneness with which he reconciled himself with life. First as a clerk, then as a civil servant (travelling in the pay of the Post Office), he had had usefully varied experience: he got to know all grades of society and to enjoy the stretch of the English scene. The geniality that he arrived at breathes, never speciously, through his novels – whose increasing success made him able to leave the Post Office and give to his new profession his full time. He wrote hard, and under prosaic conditions.

Trollope is most remembered for his clergymen: in the famous Barsetshire novels he seals up for ever the atmosphere and the personalities of an English cathedral town. He immortalized also English squires, peers, professional people and politicians. Also, I know few writers better than Trollope at conveying the charm of a charming scene. Many of his comedy characters – for instance, the incorrigible Bertie of *Barchester Towers* – are first rate. He can – as in *The Warden* – at once honour and analyse the English conscience at its most austere. He has the merit of being a very masculine writer. If he fought shy of passion, he created women who could inspire it: he puts the English heroine back on the map again; his young women are lovely, ardent, intelligent, capable, true. In some of them – especially Mary Thorne – the gallant spirit once more appears. After several early tries at the novel, Trollope arrived with *The Warden* (1855). The rest of the Barsetshire novels followed. He embarked with *Phineas Finn* (1869) on a political series – less well known now because less well done: Disraeli was far better in this genre. In *Can You Forgive Her?* (1864) he tackled the subject of erring womanhood. Before he died he had written sixty novels in all.

The Brontë genius remains a phenomenon of all, not only of English, literature. Haworth vicarage, exposed on the wilds of Yorkshire, was the home of this family: pilgrims now gaze around the vicarage as though the force of the Brontë living must have left its mark on these darkish walls. The Rev. Patrick Brontë had come from the North of Ireland: of his marriage, in 1812, there were six children – two daughters who died at a boarding-school for the daughters of clergymen, then Charlotte (1816), Patrick Branwell, Emily (1818), Anne (1820). By 1822 the family were motherless: poverty, isolation, very delicate health made up the medium of their existences. As children they roamed the moors. Charlotte went for some time to the school – the Lowood of *Jane Eyre* – that had killed her sisters. Branwell – a character so sinister that he started a darker part of the Brontë legend – took drugs, wasted money and kept the family feeling at burning point. The sisters went out as governesses: Charlotte and Emily, in order to learn languages, attached themselves for a time to the Pensionnat Heger, in Brussels. In 1846 the three sisters together published *Poems by Currer, Ellis and Acton Bell*. Charlotte's first novel, *The Professor*, failed to find a publisher, but in 1847 *Jane Eyre*, 'by Currer Bell', appeared. And in that same year came *Wuthering Heights* by the 'Ellis Bell' who was Emily. Anne Brontë published two gentler novels, *Agnes Grey* and *The Tenant of Wildfell Hall*. By the close of 1849 Branwell, Emily and Anne were dead – it was a wonder that they had lived so long. Charlotte, in that year, published *Shirley*; *Villette*, a reconstruction of *The Professor*, appeared in 1853. A year later she married her father's curate, but she was to die in 1855. *The Professor* was published after her death. Old Mr Brontë was left alone at Haworth: none of his children had reached the age of forty.

But it is an ageless fire that burns in the novels the Brontës left. The sisters were young chiefly in having lost none of their vehemence; they were involved with little outside themselves – only Charlotte at all came to terms with life. Emily, having consumed her own lonely experience, translated experience to an unearthly plane. *Wuthering Heights* is a book of fire and ice: no book has ever been better named. It is raged through, as by a wind, by a damned soul – the fated, fatal Heathcliff. The love in it is relentless, as pure of hope as it is of flesh. The house is solitary, exposed . . . here is the real English dark tower of passion above all rationality. All the same, the material setting is circumstantial; the story is full of pictures stored in Emily's living eye – the feathers plucked from the pillow, the two children in the tree in the wind. The Thrushcross firelight, with its domestic promise, by contrast darkens the darkness that is the lovers' home. And the love of Heathcliff and Catherine gains in poetic intensity by being set back inside a complex prosaic form – much of the narrative is in the idiom of 'ordinary' people; the consternation of limited people frames the unlimited tragedy.

Wuthering Heights bears no definite feminine stamp – though perhaps only a woman could have liberated her spirit so completely. Charlotte Brontë's *Jane Eyre*, on the other hand, gains force by being woman from beginning to end. Made in this voice, the plain, proud, unhesitating assertion of woman's feeling for man – Jane's for Rochester – shocked the England of 1847. It had been the accepted idea that, while woman might, by very judicious degrees, respond to declared love, she did not initiate love on her own account – to do so was more than doubtful, it was 'unwomanly'. So *Jane Eyre*, in spite of its actually faultless morals, took on an odour of impropriety – which is not to say that it was not read. If Jane, the plain little sprite of a governess, does not court her employer Rochester, she challenges him in Cleopatra's voice: their scene in the July dusk of the garden is unforgettable. Jane wants much more than love; she wants human fullness of life – the book voiced, for the first time, woman's demand for this. Read the scene where, alone on the roof of the country house, Jane looks out over the country and cries for movement, achievement, adventure – feeling the masculine part of her spirit stir. Might this be called the first feminist novel? The nature of her struggle with Rochester, who, when his existing marriage has been discovered, wants her to be his mistress, shows the hundred years' difference between Jane and Clarissa. But Jane, like Clarissa Harlowe, still identifies virtue with the power to keep her fate in her own hands. . . . *Jane Eyre*, set nearer to every-day life than *Wuthering Heights*, has a few social improbabilities in which the Brontë lack of worldly experience shows. Temperamental black-whiskered Rochester may fall a prey to our laughter; the black-souled Heathcliff never does. Charlotte Brontë, naïve, starved of beauty and luxury, rather over-describes gilded scenes – the drawing-room lit for a party, the harpy charmer's veneer. But there is something endearing about this weakness of hers. In *Shirley* she also portrays glamour – the glamour of Shirley's dashing temperament. After *Jane Eyre*, *Villette* – with its foreign atmosphere of waxed floors and cold windows, the romantic rigidity of the boarding school – is her best book. . . . At a time when male approval, coupled with money, gave woman the only status she had, it is remarkable that the only giant novels should have been written by spinster daughters of an obscure indigent clergyman.

After the Brontës, George Eliot – really Mary Ann Evans – may seem opaque and pedestrian. Not for nothing did she assume a masculine name. Her intellect must be honoured – it is more constructive than brilliant – her emotion is gravely coloured by it. She was at grips with the problems of her day. If not an attractive, she was a great, woman: as an artist she is never to be despised. Born in 1819, daughter of a land-agent, she, in helping her father with his business, early took a hand in practical life. Courageous in her emotions, she lived for years in free union with George Henry Lewes – not the least of a group of advanced thinkers to whom her propensities had attracted her. Experience had made her know many people; imagination made her penetrate them. Provincial-Midland-England is the scene of her best books – and, above all, she knew the yeoman class. She had her own sense of beauty – best seen in *Middlemarch* (1871), *Scenes from Clerical Life* (1858), and *The Mill on the Floss* (1860). She had humour, but is greatest in tragedy, which with her is found more in character (with its misuse or vain sacrifices of will) than in fate. *Felix Holt the Radical* was, in 1866, the rather stark intellectual high-point of her career. For the emotional interest one expects from a novel she is best in *Adam Bede* (1859) and *Silas Marner* (1861). She can write with a faultless convincingness, and with a noble sweep of imagination – apart from this, her books, with their palpable truth to life, are important as documents of their day.

All the same, in my heart I prefer Mrs Gaskell – as sincere a person, a less major artist and a more feminine soul. Born in 1810, she had been a beautiful Chelsea girl, reared on a succession of country visits. She married a Unitarian minister and lived, worked and felt with him in Manchester, among 'the dark satanic mills'. Her reaction to the injustices she found in industrial England of that day was of the heart, but was ruled by her steady head: unlike Dickens, she never overpainted; truth seemed to her good and bad, enough. She never lost her love – and perhaps her nostalgia – for the sweet, the comely, the orderly, the agreeable, though these, to warrant her love, must be founded on moral right. Happy in her own life as a woman, she was keenly aware of injustices done to her sex in the name of morality – she wrote her bold *Ruth* in 1853. Before this had come *Mary Barton, a Tale of Manchester Life* (1848), which is a document of the Chartist year. Called the first 'labour' novel, it prays for improved understanding between masters and men. *North and South* is much in the same vein. *Cranford*, that delicious idyll of gentility, appeared the same year as *Ruth* – to which it is a counterpoise. It is *Cranford*, with its immortal old ladies, that keeps Mrs Gaskell's name so widely known and loved in the world. Reading *Cranford* after Jane Austen's *Emma* – that other picture of an enclosed society – one is conscious of the change there had been in England in the forty years between those two books. Emma Woodhouse's Highbury is unthreatened; Miss Matty's Cranford is not – behind its orderly, small-town silence one feels vibrations from 'Drumble' – the not distant out-spreading Manchester. . . . In the *Wives and Daughters* she did not live to finish (she died in 1865) Mrs Gaskell returns to the Southern scene. With these four Victorian women writers we seem to come to the close of a period: we pass from the Mid-Victorian to the Late. The change is, rather, in attitude: the actual dates of authors overlap.

Several of George Meredith's novels, for instance, were contemporaries of George Eliot's and his first, *The Shaving of Shagpat*, appeared only nine years after *Wuthering Heights*. He was born in 1828 – and was to live on into our century. He was of Welsh extraction, and went to a Moravian school in Wales: his grandfather had been a successful tailor – a fact that was to be dug up by those enemies who accused him of snobbery (there was something less arid than snobbery in Meredith's love of the truly grand). On his return from school to London he became a solicitor's clerk, but published his first *Poems* (containing *Love in a Valley*) in 1851. These drew the attention, and later the friendship, of Rossetti and Swinburne to the brilliant young man. In fact, he was able to develop his talents in an atmosphere that was most propitious to them. He became the first English novelist with a conscious aesthetic – this may account for the *hauteur* of his style – and, more, he had a philosophy, as opposed to a general theory of right and wrong.

His poetry provides the key to his novels. Able to leave the solicitor's office for journalism, Meredith, from his room in Rossetti's house, wrote only for papers whose reputation did nothing to damage his promising name. Grub Street never really impinged on him. His first marriage failed: in 1864, one year after his second, he went to live at Flint Cottage, Box Hill, Surrey, which remained his home for the rest of his long life.

As a novelist Meredith has been found obscure, besides being a little too unaware of the banal side of human experience. The complex content of his prose does sometimes choke it – his poetry, on the other hand, continues to burn with intellectual vision. It has been argued that he should have kept to poetry. But his poems – culminating in *Modern Love* and *The Woods of Westermain* – are essentially those of a novelist. And without his novels, his smashing intellectual humour, his capricious descriptions would have been lost. Perhaps as a novelist he suffers from having lived too much in an eclectic world – unlike Thackeray, Dickens, Trollope, he can seldom have been mortified or bored. He tends to precipitate his characters – who are themselves, from their start in his brain, dynamic – into rather too special an atmosphere. His novels are, in a sense, too like operas.

All the same, it was Meredith who produced that almost faultless novel *The Egoist* (1879), in which the best of the English comedy spirit flowers – at once satirical and rotund. The plot? – a high-minded baronet is more truly, less kindly seen by a young lady than was Sir Charles Grandison. Here, too, Meredith perfects, in the best tradition, a purely English scene.

(left) *Charlotte Brontë: a portrait in crayons by George Richmond, given by Charlotte's publisher and friend George Smith to her father, the Reverend Patrick Brontë.*

(below left) *George Eliot (Mary Ann Evans) in 1865. G. H. Lewes, with whom George Eliot lived for twenty-four years in defiance of conventional morality, kept this portrait beside him in his study.*

(below right) *Elizabeth Gaskell, by George Richmond. As well as her novels, among the first to deal with the industrial scene, Mrs Gaskell wrote a biography of Charlotte Brontë, whom she met in 1850.*

One might say that his scenes are more likely, on the whole, than his characters – these, though vivid, being at times out of drawing. His sense of heroic promise in people is shadowed by his sense of their weaknesses: 'We are betrayed by what is false within.' He adored love, and shows it as adorable – all the same, he sees it as an ordeal – his early *The Ordeal of Richard Feverel* (1859) even takes its title from this idea. His stories about the youngness of young men deal with evolution rather than with adventure. Sometimes he applies his vision to politics, to national aspiration, to the international scene: some of his novels range far abroad. His heroines move through Olympian air: one charge against them has been that they talk too much. In his famous *Diana of the Crossways* (1885) he undertakes the defence of a noble creature. *Evan Harrington* (1861), *Rhoda Fleming* (1865), *Vittoria* (1867), *Beauchamp's Career* (1876), *The Amazing Marriage* (1895) also stand high with Meredith readers. He may be attacked, but he cannot be overlooked: I feel certain that he will stand the test of time.

Samuel Butler belongs in this period from having been born in 1835. His reputation, however, has been cumulative, and his importance continues to grow to-day. Grandson of the great bishop of that same name, he, on leaving Cambridge, renounced the intention of taking holy orders and went out to New Zealand, to sheep-farm. Successful in this, he also began to write. Returning to London he took up painting, and exhibited at the Royal Academy. It was in 1872 that he published his satire *Erewhon* – which has been likened to *Gulliver's Travels*. Butler might, indeed, be called the nineteenth-century Swift – comprehensive, at once enraged and precise. Grievance – his whole bent was to science, but he held himself to be boycotted by a group of accredited scientists – at once warped him and steeled his curious power. He has many aspects, but comes into the scope of this book because of his one novel, *The Way of All Flesh*. He began this in 1872; he laid it aside in 1885 – and it was not published till 1903. It is at once a hate-charged and scientific analysis of English middle-class family life (as embodied in the Pontifex family), especially of the relationship between parents and children, and its effects. It was well for the English eighteen-seventies and 'eighties, with their placid system of family reverence, that *The Way of All Flesh*, though in their time being written, was held up and did not explode on them. 1903 was quite soon enough. *The Way of All Flesh*, coming just when it did, has inspired a whole school of iconoclast novels.

Thomas Hardy was born, near the Dorchester he was to rechristen Casterbridge, in 1840, twelve years after Meredith. These two Late-

Family Prayers: *a painting by Samuel Butler, closely based on memories of his father reading prayers to the household. This picture could well serve as an illustration to Butler's autobiographical novel* The Way of All Flesh *(1903), a bitterly funny account of an upbringing in a hypocritical ecclesiastical family.*

Victorian novelists have in common that they were both poets. But while Meredith might be called a magnificent by-product of the English genius, Hardy is a figure in its direct line. In fact, his is a figure in which many tendencies culminate. The strangeness of his novels – a strangeness as great, at times, as that of *Wuthering Heights* – is counterpoised by their pervasive physical naturalness. He was England's first regional novelist – setting his stories in a tract he called Wessex, that centres on his own county of Dorsetshire. But whereas other regional novelists simply use, Hardy created, local colour: he confers a sort of super-existence on the region he wrote about. It would be true to say that Hardy did for his part

Thomas Hardy, painted by William Strang in 1893, when he was beginning work on his final and most bleak novel, Jude the Obscure.

of England what Scott had done for the Border. But a whole extension of complex human experience lies between the two. Scott's country people are walking traditions; Hardy's are sharply individualized: there is not one 'type' in the whole of his gallery. Scott revived the dignity of the past; Hardy, although the past works in him, is moved by a philosophic consciousness of the future.

Of the hero of *The Return of the Native* (1878) he says, for instance: 'In Clym Yeobright's face could dimly be seen the typical countenance of the future. Should there be a classic period to art hereafter, its Phidias may reproduce such faces. The view of life as a thing to be put up with, replacing that zest for existence which was so intense in early civilisations, must ultimately enter so thoroughly into the constitution of the advanced races that its facial expression will be accepted as a new artistic departure. People already feel that a man who lives without disturbing a curve of feature, or setting a mark of mental concern upon himself, is too far from modern perceptiveness to be a modern type. . . . The observer's eye was arrested, not by his face as a picture, but by his face as a page; not by what it was but what it recorded. His features were attractive in the light of symbols. . . .' 'The view of life as a thing to be put up with' – what a long way the human spirit had travelled by the time Hardy wrote that. There is, throughout his feeling for nature, the same sublime awareness of an endurance. Egdon Heath, in the timeless November dusk, as yet crossed by no figure, occupies the first chapter of *The Return of the Native*. 'It was at present a place perfectly accordant with man's nature – neither ghastly, hateful nor ugly: neither commonplace, unmeaning or tame; but, like man, slighted and enduring, and withal singularly colossal and mysterious in its swarthy monotony.'

But meekness is no note of Hardy's characters. His young men and women, each one singularly alone, each raise a kind of cry for perfection – through intellectual or moral achievement, through love. Each one is made dynamic either by a desire or an idea. The most alive of the men are creatures of intellect; the most alive of the women are creatures of passion. But he has also created the character that is stable and philosophic – born, one might say, already half reconciled. Very often such people are very simple: old lore, inherited wisdom speak through them.

The Return of the Native (1878), *Tess of the D'Urbervilles* (1891), and *Jude the Obscure* (1896), all three of them tragedies, have been recognized as the greatest of Hardy's novels. All have their superhumanly human scenes – Eustacia tending her solitary beacon fire, Tess waking from her bridal sleep to the fatal sunrise of Stonehenge, Jude's love Sue raising her sick husband to see the sunset reflected in a bedroom mirror. Hardy's art is, above all, diverse. His comedy spirit is, therefore, august and mellow. Merry-making, weddings and village dancing, the comic charm of bravado, naïve, racy talk, the emanation of magic from a beautiful woman, the delicious negligent poise of a pretty one, the fine day and the fine fellow, the strong sweep of hope and the long sweep of open country come equally into his range. His style, sublime at its greatest, does sometimes lapse into bathos; his dialogue, at its best idiomatic, alive with natural rhythm, has reaches of stilted unlivingness. But the architecture of his novels cannot be criticized: it is beyond praise. Hardy, after a meagre education, did in fact qualify and for years practise as an architect – so from one art to another he carried sound rules. And, his conception of life being elemental the poet in him fused with the novelist. His outstanding novels, other than those I have mentioned, are: *Under the Greenwood Tree* (1872), *Far from the Madding Crowd* (1874), *The Mayor of Casterbridge* (1886), *The Woodlanders* (1887).

England cannot really claim Henry James, though he claimed England by coming to live here and becoming in 1916 a naturalized Englishman. An American, born in New York State in 1843, he became, while still a young man, familiar with what was civilized in both hemispheres. In their high, wise kind of sophistication, his novels are cosmopolitan. At the same time, he keeps, in his observations, the alert austerity of the pioneer. He writes at once with the detachment of a spectator and the close-upness of someone under a spell. He might be called the analyst of civilization – and from this point of view England, with it enigmas, its inconsistencies, its puzzling, superb survivals, fascinated him. And, as a novelist, he was fascinated by the phenomenon of the English conscience. His affinities, as an artist in writing, were to artists abroad – Flaubert, Turgeniev – but he was to crown England, at the close of one century and the start of another, with a series of novels that penetrated to the essential Englishness of her scene. One might say that she had not been so completely perceived before.

One may say that James's perceptions only worked in the particular area of his social tastes. He had an aesthetic love of the *beau monde* – whether it be of artists or aristocrats. As in Meredith's case, desire attracted him to the people and settings of which he wrote. Any character in a Henry James story or novel, however low his or her stated class in life, is promoted – by being made articulate or susceptible – to his or her place in James's *beau monde*. And he makes the same promotions in age as he does in class: even his children are, in their fineness, mature. In a sense, his adults are child-like, in having crystalline natures. The fact was, that James could only use the *fine* nature – whether evil or good – for his very special treatment of the predicament. And predicament was his subject at every time. His sense of beauty is matched by his sense of evil: his villains do worse than oppress or threaten – they subtly and immeasurably corrupt. His innocent characters move through danger zones; the spirit is in peril, seldom the flesh. Evil only operates directly in a few of the James stories – the great example is *The Turn of the Screw*. Elsewhere, its action is indirect;

it may work through the most apparently natural affections, desires and loyalties . . . . see, for instance, *The Spoils of Poynton* (1896). In *The Golden Bowl*, with its London scene of poised and controlled cosmopolitan people, he shows the implicit rather than the conventional ugliness of an adultery. Under Henry James's adroitness, behind his complex constructions, is the simple pattern of the morality play. In the end, he sees nothing as beautiful that has not been proved good. He subjected to moral examination the grace, the privilege, the mystery, the tradition of the age-polished England he loved so well.

Henry James's great novels and stories are astoundingly many. His style became increasingly involuted; his later novels are not found easy to read.

A Rage of Wonderment: *Max Beerbohm's caricature of Henry James was prompted by a remark of the novelist's – 'no more dignity . . . than the boots and shoes we see, in the corridors of promiscuous hotels, standing, often in double pairs, at the doors of rooms' – and indicates two outstanding features of James's fiction: penetrating but detached observation and fastidious moral standards.*

William Nicholson.

Rudyard Kipling.

Rudyard Kipling: a woodcut by William Nicholson. Kipling's evocations of boyhood and of life in India, combined with calls to Britain to recognize her imperial commitments, brought him immense popularity.

His first long novel was *Roderick Hudson* (1876). Landmarks in his work have been: *The American* (1877), *Daisy Miller* (1878), *The Portrait of a Lady* (1881), *The Princess Casamassima* (1886), *The Spoils of Poynton* (1896), *What Maisie Knew* (1897), *The Two Magics* (which contains *The Turn of the Screw*) (1898), *The Awkward Age* (1899), *The Wings of the Dove* (1902), *The Ambassadors* (1903), *The Golden Bowl* (1904). Though he did not die (in England) till 1916, his great fiction period had closed years before that.

So Henry James has carried us over from the nineteenth century to our own. The same transition was made by a number of novelists whom, alas, I have no room to name here. In fact, the great Late-Victorians I have discussed were in reality far from isolated: to let them seem so gives an incomplete picture of their day. It has taken years for them to stand out from among their more popular contemporaries. I am now conscious of two very bad lacunæ in not having mentioned either George Gissing or George Moore – the first a 'straight' realist, the second an æsthete-realist, Irish, much touched by French influence, whose work has an outstanding quality. And a still graver omission is Robert Louis Stevenson, the second great Scot to influence England. In his power to raise the story of action to a heroic, sometimes poetic, level, Stevenson was to be approached by Joseph Conrad – the Polish sea captain who added to English writing a sort of fervour and glory – a temperament. I can name, in the space that is left to me, only four novelists who carry forward into, or at least touch, our own time.

There is Rudyard Kipling, for instance. The artist in him has been quite wrongly obscured, in some views, by the Imperialist. Actually, he was realistic, quite disabused, about English life abroad as well as at home. The dramatic side of the Empire did appeal to him – but he knew its plain working side well, as a journalist. He likes energy, courage, action in any form: if he salutes these in the English one cannot blame him. His best work is in the field of the short story – setting and incident interest him more than character, though his touch on character can be devastatingly sure. His long novel, *The Light that Failed*, is, though moving, on the sentimental side. No English writer has been more mobile and vivid in his depiction of action. Also, he makes one see, smell, touch what he describes: his descriptions are charged with reality. For a number of untravelled English people he has, for instance, 'created' India for ever. He has, and quite often likes to use, a real English-gothic command of the horrific. In *Plain Tales from the Hills*, and other collections, he has written some ruthless love-stories: love does not appear to Kipling to be a rational passion. Anglo–Indian life, boy life and the British Army are, in general, taken to be his province. In his children's stories he shows pure imagination in his treatment of the past and of animals. He was born in Bombay in 1865, and the publication dates of his books extend from 1881 to 1930. He has left us some classic tales of the last war.

H. G. Wells, born 1866, has, like Samuel Butler, the scientific approach to life. He applies science to the novel. Like Hardy, he has a constant sense of the future – but, whereas Hardy apprehended the future only as the extreme of a psychic state, Wells commits himself to exact material prophecies. Science has justified his predictions by already coming abreast of several of them – but the stories have their independent place in art as being magnificent fantasies. *The Time Machine*, for instance, came in 1895, *The War of the Worlds* in 1898, *The Food of the Gods* in 1904, *Men Like Gods* in 1923. It may be said that Wells's rationalized Utopias offer no place for the human soul – which, one takes it, will no longer exist. If so, in the future there will be no more great novels. . . . The Utopian novels have made great impacts: fearless, iconoclastic, impertinent from the point of view of tradition, they do always stimulate thought. But it is in consciousness of his own age, of the maladies and the aspirations of men as they are to-day – in fact, as a straightforward novelist – that Wells seems to me to excel. He has a truly Dickensian eye for the comic. *Kipps* (1905) and *The History of Mr Polly* (1910) are novels that could not be better. *Ann Veronica* (1909), *Marriage* (1912), *Joan and Peter* (1918) are milestones in the analysis of his age. Wells is at once engaged and fascinated by the impossibility of rationalizing love: sex seems to hold up progress, the way things are. Others of the novels – outstandingly, *Mr Britling Sees It Through* (1916) – fall into the document group: they crystallize the feeling and the conditions of a particular period. From the first, Wells has been liked or disliked for a particular boldness – *Tono Bungay* (1909) and *The New Machiavelli* (1911) made revolutions in their day. And the present day has not yet caught up with his thoughts: for our own generation he flies a tremendous flag.

In his move from the social novel, with its acceptances, to the sociological novel, with its attacks, Wells was accompanied by Arnold Bennett (1867–1931). But in the Bennett novels – which at their finest, for instance, *The Old Wives' Tale* (1908), stand up to anything Europe has put out – the artist towers over the man of ideas. In fact, general conditions chiefly interested Bennett in so far as they serve to explain particular lives. Like Hardy, he re-created a region – the Five Towns, in the northern Midlands, dark with the smoke of the potteries. In him appears, at its most lively, the English satiric sense – and as success closed in on his own life, how freely he satirized success! He became accomplished enough as a writer to explore every genre – the thriller, the domestic comedy. After *The Old Wives' Tale*, among his serious work comes the *Clayhanger* trilogy (1910–15), and *Riceyman's Steps* (1923). He lived years in France, loved her and learned from her the uncompromising regard that is due to art. The French æsthetic ideal – detachment – was always uppermost in his mind: to this we owe his objective view of England – as valuable in an Englishman as it is rare.

John Galsworthy's novels have not worn so well. His dates are 1867–1933. The *Forsyte Saga* novels (1906–28) have their first interest – and are much read abroad – as documents of the English upper middle class. They have the merits of all his other writing – intellectual scrupulousness, sense of beauty, a rather hopeless passion for social justice, and, with regard to women, a serious but exotic sentimentality. His pictures of men of property, men created by their sense of their own position, are more searching than Thackeray's, more fastidious than Trollope's – yet somehow the different Forsytes fail to be major figures. Possibly Galsworthy was not ruthless enough; perhaps he failed (while he did boldly attempt) to objectify the tradition in which he had been brought up. He attacks privilege, but in a privileged way. His disinterested ambitions deserve praise: one would not be so much aware of his limitations had he not attempted to do so much. As a dramatist – and he was called the English Ibsen – he learned how to give the fullest force to a scene – so it is the scenes in his novels that are remembered; one tends to lose sight of their continuity. In his sense of place he excels; he has immortalized London; he has a sensuous feeling for countrysides. His characters, with their ascetic wills, dread beauty because of its dangerous power: in fact, you could not have a fairer example than Galsworthy of one kind of English romanticism. His novels most to be recommended are: *The Man of Property* (1906), *The Patrician* (1911), *The Dark Flower* (1913), *In Chancery* (1920), *To Let* (1921).

These four writers – Kipling, Wells, Bennett and Galsworthy – have been in their time, and each in his own way, more revolutionary than any younger men. We now take for granted a great deal that they achieved. The novelist of to-day has less to react against. So we feel some break in temperament between these four last Late-Victorians and the novelists who are at their maturity to-day – for instance, Aldous Huxley, Somerset Maugham. Has there come, too, a break in the English novel tradition? Looking back, we may say that the English novelists have, from the eighteenth century up to some years ago, excelled in the creation of character, and, secondarily, in the drawing of scenes, rather than in the analysis of ideas and passions. They have left us a gallery of immortal English creatures – eccentrics, haphazard fine young men, fantasists, optimists, blackguards, silly women, dashing bad women, lovely spirited girls; they have left us English landscapes as various as ever came from the sweep of an English brush. Hardy and Meredith, poet-novelists, were the first to indicate any change.

D. H. Lawrence in New Mexico, 1923. Here, away from an England which he felt had rejected him, he sought the primitive dark forces of the unconscious, repressed in 'civilized' Europe.

There is, I think, a change now, though not a break. D. H. Lawrence has come and gone: his explosive novels have had the effect of a sort of depth-charge, bringing much to the surface. Lawrence was, it would seem, at once behind and in advance of his own time: his puritanical antipuritanism was paradoxical. In writing of worlds he knew, he commanded an admirable realism, tinged with poetry, and a simplicity that has not been praised enough; these having been obscured, for the general reader, by his 'prophetic' quality, and by his (apparent) doctrine of purification by fire – i.e., sexual passion. At any rate, D. H. Lawrence played a major part in shifting the stress from character – in which, ever since, our contemporary novelists show an interest that is much less exclusive. They continue to turn, instead, to just those ideas and passions in which individual destinies count for less, in which people take less colour from their surroundings because those surroundings change from day to day? One great war has already left, another is in the act of placing, its mark on English habit, feeling and thought. I do not think English essentials will ever change – but events make us sharply conscious of what these are. The novelist to-day must think for himself: this is no time to add random comments to life. So the English novel gains in self-consciousness – it may have lost some of the old spontaneity.

I cannot see my contemporaries as I see the earlier novelists: that is, I cannot see them down the perspective of time. They are many, and vitally on the move. To attempt to judge them would be to attempt to immobilize them. I may have been arbitrary about the dead; I will not be misleading about the living. With every day, values go up and down. So I shall close with a reference only to two modern novelists whose work seems to me to have attained a position clear of the daily critical flux. One, Virginia Woolf, is recently dead; the other, E. M. Forster, has not published a novel since 1924. These two seem to me both to epitomize English tradition and to have moved forward along lines of their own.

E. M. Forster's novels are more straightforward, more (at least apparently) in the familiar manner than those of Virginia Woolf: they have developed plots, they give place (though not the first place) to character; they have a high ironic level of comedy, and their dialogue comes abreast with Jane Austen's. What is new in them is their particular mental climate; also, the nature of other people's predicaments. Contrast does much to give these novels structure and meaning – contrast between one country, with its inherent spirit, and another (suburban England and hill-town Italy in *Where Angels Fear to Tread*, between England and India in *A Passage to India*), between convention and passion (in *A Room with a View*), between illusion and truth (in *The Longest Journey* and *Howard's End*). In each, the central character is kept at the high tension of a continuous decision. Through experience the character seems to make a journey – an often lonely destination is reached. The controlled, level style of the narration can be penetratingly beautiful.

In Virginia Woolf's novels the characters are less mobile; they seem to stand still, amazed, while experience ripples past. The men and women have an intense inner existence; each generates his or her own world. Imagination of this pure power has not been brought to narrative style

(right) *E. M. Forster in his rooms at King's College, Cambridge, photographed by Cecil Beaton. The University is the setting for important sections of his novels* The Longest Journey *(1907) and* Maurice *(1971). (below) Virginia Woolf, photographed by her husband Leonard in about 1937.*

before: Virginia Woolf has been likened to Sterne – but her imagination is less contused than his. I have not heard her compared with Emily Brontë – but Emily Brontë has been the only other woman capable of this upward sweep. While the *Wuthering Heights* setting is in itself extraordinary, Virginia Woolf's choice of setting has been the reverse, and her characters are, in their outward aspects, made almost deliberately tame. She chooses, in fact, unlikely matter to kindle – but, once kindled, how high she makes it burn! She has put behind her, having no need of, devices that make all other stories work. The towering inner strangeness of her people appears not at all in their outward actions (which appear conventional and compliant), but in the manner in which they see and feel. Only in the earliest of her novels, *The Voyage Out*, do the characters actually make a journey: they go to South America. Otherwise, they are confined to the experiences of London, the English countryside and seashore. But never before has England appeared as it appears under this burning-glass of her art. Once, in *Orlando*, she turns the glass on the English past. Otherwise, all her titles – *Night and Day, Jacob's Room, Mrs Dalloway, To the Lighthouse, The Waves, The Years, Between the Acts* – suggest the familiar 'now' – the familiar scene, in cycles of light and darkness, in hearing of the rhythm of tides. Time, not passion, spins any plot that there is – and yet Virginia Woolf has been supreme in her power to place the life art touches beyond the power of time.

I have tried, as I promised at the start of this book, to make felt the wideness of the To-day of art, and return past novelists to their place in its light. So it is fitting to close with Virginia Woolf's name: she lived as well as wrote in the presence of that To-day.

Diaries & Journals

KATE O'BRIEN

ET me begin with the hard saying that the best English diaries
have been written by bores. It will be the purpose of ensuing
pages so to illustrate, explain and modify this statement as, I
hope, to remove its sting; but for clarity's sake I must start from it as set
down above, for I believe it to be a basic truth about the greatest diarists. A
bore has been excellently defined as 'a person who mentions everything'.
'*L'art d'ennuyer c'est de tout dire*', and face to face with us, across the fireplace
or the dining table, the exponent of this art is very nearly intolerable; but
at the remove which lies between a writer and reader, when the
'everything', printed not spoken, is in our power, to be taken or left as
we feel inclined, and when distance, time, have given it patina and
perspective, he who in life might have been our plague becomes our
entertainer, and sometimes more than that – a light, a lamp, a gentle,
accidental resurrector for a while of what had been cold and dead.

And it is of course probable, indeed almost certain, that in life this
diarist, this entertainer, was *not* a bore, that he escaped the Nemesis of his
temperament by the grace of being a diarist; for it is unlikely that a man
who noted down in ink everything he saw, heard or otherwise
experienced each day over a period of years should have had the vitality or
indeed the time to recount himself to his contemporaries *verbatim* as he
does to us. So their escape is our gain; and his adaptation to script of his
perpetual need to pettifog and annotate translates the latter into positive
merit, and in some cases makes posterity and history immeasurably the
debtors of a few eccentric or fussy or over-cautious men who, but for the
chance that they scribbled rather than chattered, might have remained for
ever obscure to us – just departed bores, mercifully stemmed in the
irresponsive grave from their habit of 'running on'.

A good diary is not necessarily literature; for of its nature it must be free
of most of the disciplines and tests of a work of art. Vision, imagination,
passion, fancy, invention, scholarship, detachment, and the steely

Kate O'Brien, photographed in about 1950.

restraints and consciously selected embellishments of form and of design –
none of these has a vital place in diary-writing. They break in, it is true, or
may do so; but that they are not essential to a diarist or part of his talent is
at once his advantage and his peril – his advantage if, apart from them, he
possesses enough of the attributes his task *may* demand, for so, merely by
pleasing himself and evading all the pains of art, he will come to wear a
laurel as evergreen as Pepys'; his peril, too, because any piece of writing,
diary or what you will, can only manage to live and get itself read by
projecting somehow that illusion of life and truth which is the function of
literature. So the diarist might be in a dilemma were he self-conscious
along these lines, or posterity-conscious. But he need not worry, very
likely; for his impulse – to set down everything – proves his vitality. And
vitality, the first and the only unfakeable element of literature, is what he
needs above all else for getting read hereafter. Let him be alive, and rock-
set on reproducing for us the daily pattern made by his own liveliness – an
odd necessity, you may say, in any really lively person, but that is
irrelevant – and ten to one you will get a good diary. History and its
ironies, the eternal nostalgia of readers and their simple curiosity – all will
do for his pages what the creative artist would have had to do for them
himself; and out of a minimum of effort and a maximum of self-
indulgence, something which is almost a work of art may be observed to
grow, to have grown.

  In the simplicity therefore with which the typical English diarist sets
out to capture on paper the busy to and fro of his earthly span lies the
threat of his being by nature a bore. For, if we except journals kept in
special circumstances – as for instance in the course of perilous
explorations such as Captain Scott's, or say Wesley's enormous and
businesslike record of his missions – there is something a touch complacent
and niggling in the design. And it is true that so far as we know almost no
really great man has been in the normal course of his life a consistent diary-
keeper. André Gide is a curious exception, and we must hope that he is still
industriously and resolutely proving the rule – for our future
enlightenment and delight. And we shall never know what journals and
notebooks many of the great have had the wit, or the folly, to throw into
the fire. But, as the records stand and as the diaries have come down to us,
they are provedly not a form of self-expression which has appealed to the
richly endowed. They are the medium of secondary types, as a rule – the
outlet of the modest, the orderly and, sometimes, the complacent.

  And they are none the worse for that. Indeed, paradoxically, their greatness, or more accurately, their great value lies now in their littleness, their concern with the passing day and the particular – the price of a dish of Tongue and Udder, the effect of a rhubarb purge, the writing of a postcard. Diarists have found such matters worth the setting down – which means that had they not set them down they would have pestered their contemporaries with them – and been bores of the kind we all know, who labour the obvious, and teach grandmother to suck eggs.

Trivia of custom, of gossip or of comment could not of themselves, of course, sustain a diary, or give it importance; but the diarist's necessity of writing them down places them, willy-nilly, in relation to large things and gives them as it were their function of accent or balance in the composition of a period; time itself heightens this function; and in the greater diaries the writer, managing to relate his very self to his notes and his doings, managing actually to express his own life, however modest or however brilliant, in just proportion to his time, does arrive, even if haphazardly, at creating one kind of work of art. So we may fall upon the irony of the little man of little talent and less ambition accomplishing, in conspiracy with time, such strokes of illumination, of irony or of sheer, true life as the great imaginative ones have always had to wrestle for in uncertainty and pain, and with all their faculties on the stretch. Thus it is, perhaps, when Nancy Woodforde writes down, as dully and smugly as possible, on Friday September 28th, 1792, in a Norfolk parsonage: 'Mr and Mrs Custance sent us a brace of partridges. Dreadful times in France. Many are fled for refuge here.' That placid entry shows us as neatly as it could be done how wide and green and safely misted were then as for a long time afterwards the miles that lay between historic inevitabilities and that constant of rural England, the provincial lady. And when Francis Kilvert writes, on March 7th, 1873: 'As I walked home across the meadows the sun was sinking low. In the clear beautiful evening a bird-hunting boy with a light heart was singing at the top of his voice across the fields. I only caught snatches of the verses. It seemed to be a love-song, and he repeated the same lines again and again. When he had ended his song the boy relieved his feelings by a shout and then sang "Saturday Night is soon a-coming" ' – we have a particular spring evening, its sound, its stillness, its essence, related – by a boy's voice across a field – to a hundred such evenings we have known. For that is one thing the diary, at its best, can do – not merely inform us about life, but, by chance fusion of some inner or outer facet of it with what we also know or feel, make us recognize it.

If I seem arbitrary in the pages that follow, I hope I shall be forgiven; for I take my task to be the pleasant one of discussing my own preferences and dislikes among diarists, rather than gravely and detachedly to compose a concise history of the diary. I shall skip, I shall ignore; perhaps, should any such glance my way, I shall get into trouble with a scholar or two; and indeed it might save time for some readers were I forthwith to put my cards on the table and, since what I am about to write will be no more than a record of personal taste, confess at once my chief reaction to the most celebrated of all diaries? But no – let us begin at the beginning, and hold as nearly as we can to the only order it is practicable to impose on so brief a sketch of a vastly diversified minor art – a loosely chronological one. Let us for simplicity's sake review English diarists and their diaries century by century, as they come.

The English Diary proper seems to have made its first appearance in the seventeenth century. Sir William Dugdale, an industrious Warwickshire gentleman, who laboured all his long life at works of antiquarianism and of heraldry and fought for Charles I in the Civil War, kept a journal during the latter forty-five of his eighty-two years of life which, dull, dry and broken as it is, the merest jotting indeed – 'Queene impeached of Treason. Two regiment of foote came from York to Newark.' 'Two sunnes appeared this day.' 'King Charles the 2nd departed this life, about noon.' – does build up, slow stroke by stroke, a portrait of a man. A dull man, unremarkable, inarticulate, hide-bound, yet one faithful alike to his duties and to his interests, having unity in him, and with his conventions tempered by a carefully ordered individualism. In fact, from dry, modest notes never intended for publication, notes localized and made small by the writer's phlegmatic temperament even when they touch on large events, we get a reliable portrait – neither inspired nor grossly out of drawing, but merely faithful – of the English country gentleman as he has persisted through three hundred years. Domestic and orderly as well as conventional and idiosyncratic – for Sir William's very last note is simply this: 'Payd Elizabeth Taylor for her Quarter's Wages, now ended, and she going away from us . . .'. It is an entry we are to read again and again through the diaries of three hundred years. But Sir William also left us this hearsay note, for January 30th, 1649: 'The King beheaded at the gate of Whitehalle . . . His head was thrown downe by him yt tooke it up; bruised ye face. His haire cut of. Souldiers dipped their swords in his blood. Base language uppon his dead body.'

John Evelyn: an engraving by R. Nanteuil of 1650, when the diarist was thirty.
His diary contains detailed accounts of political and social events between 1641 and 1706.
Pepys paid him a measured compliment: 'a most excellent person he is, and must be allowed a
little for a little conceitedness, but he may be so, being a man so much above others'.

When very near the end of his life, this modest diarist crossed with a
greater, and thus got his name recorded in such a full and broad-flung
journal as he could never have attempted. For May 21st, 1685, John
Evelyn begins his entry: 'I dined at my Lord Privy Seal's, with Sir
William Dugdale, Garter King-at-Arms, author of the *Monasticon* and
other learned works; he told me he was 82 years of age and had his sight
and memory perfect . . .'.

John Evelyn was a man so gifted, so prosperous, so balanced, so long-
lived, so popular, so sane and so naturally self-confident that the average
human being may be forgiven if he turns from the bright prospect with
something like a shudder. 'A strain of innocent gaiety and refined
enjoyment marks Evelyn's life from first to last', says one commentator.
'Innocent gaiety' is an attractive phrase, but it is open to the neutral reader
of the great journal to question its accuracy in description of the
gentlemanly shrewdness, the balanced worldliness, which dominate John
Evelyn's every page. For my own part, while conceding the 'refined

enjoyment', of which there is a remarkable plenty, I withhold the former tribute as too free and luminous for what it praises. It is captious, maybe, to quarrel however mildly with eighty-five years lived so gracefully, on a high level of learning, taste, piety, good temper and tolerance – yet one cannot but feel that Evelyn's life opened more sweetly and freely, and in greater spiritual and individual promise, than he later understood, or looked for. In 1641, when he was twenty-one, he began the diary which he was to keep with fidelity during sixty-four full and exemplary years; but in the opening pages he sketches in briefly his birth and parentage, and the scenes and major events of his childhood; and from these first passages we get hints of carelessness, of temperamental eccentricities and difficulties in the boy which were to disappear from the worldly, balanced record of the man – 'I was now . . . put to nurse to one Peter, a neighbour's wife and tenant, of a good, comely, brown, wholesome complexion, and in a most sweet place towards the hills, flanked with wood and refreshed with streams; the affection to which kind of solitude I sucked in with my very milk.' True, in part; and becoming a great gardener and horticulturist, he remained always attracted to the more civilized beauties of rural life, and even protested sometimes his yearning for 'recess', as in a letter to Cowley : '. . . should think myself more happy than crowned heads were I, as you, the arbiter of mine own life, and could break from those gilded toys . . . '. But no man has ever been more than Evelyn the arbiter of his own life, and all his writings calmly set out his polite but obstinate pre-occupation with the 'gilded toys'.

As a schoolboy, he begged off Eton, being 'unreasonably terrified with the report of the severe discipline there', and was schooled, very indifferently, in Wotton village and at Lewes, taking 'so extraordinary a fancy to drawing and designing that I could never after wean my inclinations from it, to the expense of much precious time . . .'. At Oxford he seems, by his own account, to have wasted his time, save that he 'began to look upon the rudiments of music, in which I afterwards arrived to some formal knowledge'; and in the Middle Temple he was plainly bored with the law, 'that impolished study'. So that when, in his twenty-first year, he lost his father, he felt a great anxiety and chill in bereavement, and described himself as being at that time 'of a raw, vain, uncertain and very unwary inclination . . . who now thought of nothing but the pursuit of vanity, and the confused imaginations of young men'.

Such he was then, in the year of his own majority and of the beginning of Charles the First's bitter struggle against Parliament. When we place these simple and interesting admissions beside what we know of his unusual natural talents, the quickness and ease of his mind, the diversity and excellence of his interests, and when we add that he was rich, free, well-born and honourable, it can be agreed that he was a young man of immense potentialities. Anything might come of the alliance of so many positive endowments with the temperamental diffidences, vanities, curiosities and 'confused imaginations' to which their possessor has confessed. We recall, when we survey the brilliant, dangerous sum of this young man, William Windham, of whose intermittent diary-keeping we shall have occasion to speak later on. But Windham, always conscious of frustration and of the seeds of failure in himself, would have understood, in application to his own soul, Shelley's line about 'the contagion of the world's slow stain'; whereas Evelyn so conditioned and governed himself that it is probable that the relation of such a phrase to his bright and safe maturing would have struck him as sheer nonsense.

Yet the contagion of the world, of his own concern for the world and for having the best of it, did somehow blight his life, making it neatly perfect, like the gardens he cherished, instead of free and incalculable, as it could have been. He took a curious decision in 1642-3 – curious, that is, for the man who two hundred years later was to be celebrated in *John Inglesant* as the flower of the Cavalier type. Here it is, in his own words: 'The 12th November was the Battle of Brentford, surprisingly fought; and to the great consternation of the City, had his Majesty (as it was believed he would) pursued his advantage. I came in with my horse and arms just at the retreat; but was not permitted to stay longer than the 15th, by reason of the army marching to Gloucester; which would have left both me and my brothers exposed to ruin, without any advantage to his Majesty. . . . on the 10th (December) returned to Wotton, nobody knowing of my having been in his Majesty's army . . . 12th July, I sent my black menage horse and furniture with a friend to his Majesty, at Oxford. 23rd, The Covenant being pressed, I absented myself; but, finding it impossible to evade the doing very unhandsome things . . . October the 2nd I obtained a licence of his Majesty, dated at Oxford and signed by the King, to travel again.' Thus in November 1643, aged twenty-three and unencumbered, he left England, and stayed away for four years. He returned, a newly married man, but leaving his wife in Paris, in September 1647, 'to settle may affairs'; stayed for eighteen months, settled into Sayes Court in Deptford, bought and sold manors and works of art, sat for his portrait, studied chemistry, and kept his ear well to the ground in the political scene. 'I got privately into the council of the rebel army at Whitehalle, where I heard horrid villainies.' 'The villainy of the rebels proceeding now so far as to try, condemn and murder our excellent King . . . struck me with such horror that I kept the day of his martyrdom a fast, and would not be present at that execrable wickedness . . .'. Six months after the King's execution Evelyn rejoined his wife in Paris, and except for one brief trip home in 1650, stayed abroad until the spring of 1652. He then settled at Deptford, and arranged for his wife to come to England, being advised by his friends 'to compound with the soldiers'. Whence may be said to have begun the full flow of that settled, correct, domestic, scholarly, social and altogether perfect life, which was to run without heat or quarrel and with scarcely a sorrow, scarcely an anxiety, into the beginning of the reign of Anne.

He had decided, at twenty-three, on caution, and on attending to his own interests. Not, so far as we can discover, out of intellectual contempt for the mess his country was in, and not out of lack of interest in the general situation – but simply for selfish reasons. Perhaps he was right. In any case, his decision served him well, and no one ever sought to penalize his curious tepidity. 'He must have conducted himself with uncommon prudence, and address,' writes his first editor, William Bray, in 1818, 'for he had personal friends in the Court of Cromwell at the same time that he was corresponding with his father-in-law, Sir Richard Browne, the ambassador of King Charles II at Paris . . . His manners we may presume to have been the most agreeable; for his company was sought by the greatest men . . . He was happy in a wife of congenial disposition with his own, of an enlightened mind . . . though he remained a decided Royalist, he managed so well as to have intimate friends even amongst those nearly connected with Cromwell; and to this we may attribute his being able to avoid taking the Covenant, which he says he never did take . . .'.

Thomas Hardy's cottage at Higher Brockhampton, Dorset, at the heart of the country that he called Wessex. Here Hardy was born in 1840, here he lived for most of the first thirty years of his life, and here he wrote Under the Greenwood Tree *(1872) – where the cottage appears as Tranter Dewey's house – and* Far From the Madding Crowd *(1874). A path near the cottage leads to Egdon Heath, the bleak expanses of which provide the setting for* The Return of the Native *(1878).*

(overleaf) 'High Withens' on Haworth Moor, believed by friends of the Brontës to be the model for Wuthering Heights. *It certainly answers to Emily Brontë's description of the high, stormy situation of the Heights, 'completely removed from the stir of society'.*

(left) *The eighteenth-century Monks House, in the village of Rodmell near Lewes, Sussex, was discovered by Leonard and Virginia Woolf in the summer of 1919; it became their permanent country home and here Virginia worked on many of her novels, beginning with* Jacob's Room *(1922).*

(below) *8a Victoria Street, Eastwood, the small house in a hill-top town in the Nottinghamshire coalfield, where D. H. Lawrence was born in 1885.* Sons and Lovers, *his first major work, is a semi-autobiographical account of his upbringing in these surroundings.*

(overleaf) *The Boathouse at Laugharne on the South Wales coast where Dylan Thomas lived for four and a half years before his death in 1953. Here he wrote his radio-play* Under Milk Wood, *a comic and poetic portrait of life in a small Welsh coastal town not unlike Laugharne.*

Tolerance and tact are excellent things, but it is impossible not to regret the excess of them which we find in Evelyn, and their alliance to self-interest; for passion, that warmth in a man which, even in his mistakes, may make him the friend of his fellowmen and a part of their humanity, could have been nobly mettled by all the gifts which Evelyn preferred to harness to decorum and to social ease. He might have been a leader of his age; he was instead one of its most fixed and untarnished decorations. He wrote a great deal, on politics, on Jesuitism, on the Navy, on Sculpture, on Engraving, on Forestry, Agriculture, and Horticulture. He was linguist, scientist, and amateur of the arts. He helped to found the Royal Society; and after the Restoration he sat on various Royal Commissions. In all these undertakings he excelled, as also in his duties as husband, father and landowner; and he lived and died a devout, untroubled Christian. All this, and very much more, we learn from his vast diary, which is an incomparably informative, full picture of a society and an era. It gives us everything that the observant Evelyn saw and touched upon in eighty-five years – except the passions, the urgencies, the doubts, despairs and sins of men, or of one man. The external symptoms of these elements may be touched upon, but only to be banked down by conventional pieties or – when for instance he describes the Fire of London, so admirably, so vividly – with a detachment that is just a shade too cold, too touched with carefulness. '. . . blessing and adoring the distinguishing mercy of God to me and mine, who in the midst of all this ruin, was like Lot, in my little Zoar, safe and sound'. 'Still the plague continuing in our parish, I could not, without danger, adventure to our church.' 'This night was acted my Lord Broghill's tragedy, called *Mustapha*, before their Majesties at Court, at which I was present . . . I was invited by my Lord Chamberlain . . . though in my mind I did not approve of any such pastime in a time of such judgments and calamities.'

He was too great a man to be so priggish and careful; too intellectually gifted to hunt so consistently with the hares while he ran with the hounds. But he has left us a splendid panorama, crowded but clear, of a time in English history which was packed with events, with troubles and with

Thoor Ballylee, near Gort in County Galway, is a sixteenth-century castle keep beside a river bridge. It was bought by W. B. Yeats in 1917 shortly after his marriage and restored as a summer home. In 'Meditations in Time of Civil War' he describes how 'The bees build in the crevices | Of loosening masonry, and there | The mother birds bring grubs and flies.' Bees still have a nest outside his window.

development. As a man, measured by his own powers and opportunities, he is disappointing; but as a diarist he is invaluable.

His friend, Samuel Pepys, a distinguished public servant, kept a diary too – though only for nine years, instead of sixty-five; and this diary which, it seems clear enough, was never intended for any other eyes besides its writer's, has become the most famous in the world. Everyone knows about it, and most people have read it, or read in it. Pepys began to keep it on 1st January, 1660, when he was twenty-seven years old, and just about to be appointed a Clerk of the Acts in the Navy Office; he was a married man, having in 1655 espoused a young lady of Huguenot extraction; he was of gentle birth and had been educated at St Paul's and at Cambridge; he was industrious, lively, talented, and had influential friends; his major desires were to get on in life, to do his work dutifully, and to enjoy himself. Trouble with his eyes compelled him to abandon his diary at the end of May, 1669. He died in 1703, at the age of seventy. In the course of his public life he was Clerk of the Privy Seal, Secretary to the Admiralty, Member of Parliament, President of the Royal Society and Master of Trinity House. Once, because of his loyalty to his chief, the Duke of York, he was charged with implication in the Papist Plot, and sent to prison. He was a friend of Dryden, of Evelyn and of many distinguished persons. He was interested in literature and in the theatre; particularly he was interested in music, and was generous and kind to musicians. He liked to dress well, to eat well and to be in on the talk of the town; he liked to dally with women, and to live contentedly with his wife, to control her extravagances, and to see her pretty and happy. He worried about money; he took an interest in his house and its decoration; he collected a library, gave musical parties and was sociable; he fussed about his health, and every 26th March he piously celebrated his having been successfuly 'cut for the stone' on that day in 1658; he worked very hard and was trustworthy and scrupulous, staying at his post in London, for instance, all through the panic of the Great Plague. He was, in short, the type, the prototype of the English higher Civil Servant – and he appears to have succeeded better than many such in gratifying his natural ambitions, public and private.

The Diary proves and supports the external story. It does so by the paradoxical method of turning it upside down, or inside out, and revealing to us that the basic man on whom this other, this watchful, educated, diplomatic, honest, anxious keeper-up of appearances, is founded is in fact that other's antithesis – naïve, ignorant, reckless, shy, a taker of the silliest risks, a bewildered victim of himself, the creature of his petty impulses, a man forever in danger from his own instabilities and inconsistencies. What could be more interesting, consoling or alarming for any of us to read? Who is there who has not shuddered to imagine some sudden impossible revelation to the world of his actual self – not the self of this very high or that inexpressibly low moment, but the true small self that frets and chugs along relentlessly, in time with our outward gestures and grimaces? The self *we* know, but which, while we alternately inflate and enjoy it, or miserably writhe against its monstrous embrace, we are least determined no one else shall come within miles of knowing? Pepys has, as nearly as any man ever, brought off this dreadful, unnatural feat – of presenting his whole self, stark naked, quite defenceless, to his fellowmen. No wonder he is an immortal. He has done it very well too – working his whole self, all he is, all his most pitiful and true *minutiae*, into a bright, close, restless picture of London and Court Society during a time that was unusually vivid and loose, unusually dangerous, exciting and worth observation. The story he tells is packed with characters and stories, overflowing with plums for historian and gossip – but he is his own central theme, and he does not mislay himself. Naïve, chattering, and childishly fussed to catch in everything, he gives us, as we say, the works. '. . . My mind, God forgive me, too much running upon what I can *ferais avec la femme de Bagwell demain* . . .'. So on, so on; Krupp and Pierce and Mercer and The. Turner and poor Deb; and all the small sins, ailments and sensations of the common day; all the humiliations of our wretched, silly flesh. 'Here I did *ce que je voudrais avec* her most freely, and it having cost me 2s. in wine and cake upon her, I away sick of her impudence, and by coach to my Lord Brunker's.' It is an astonishing and, in the full and serious meaning of the word, a shocking achievement.

Perhaps it is somewhat *too* shocking. For my own part, I have never liked Pepys' diary; I have found that a very little of it goes a mighty long way, and at that leaves me bored. To have dared so much for so tiny a result; to empty out breast, brain and entrails, and have so wretchedly little to show for the awful violence; to be, after all and with all said, nothing better or worse than fussy, kindly, nervous, lecherous, dirty, self-pitying and respectable! To be in fact inside, after all the drama of confession, exactly what the outside advertised – no more and no less! That is Pepys – as no doubt it is all of us. And if so, there is the strength and merit of his diary. Yet one must be forgiven for not liking it. It is amusing, but not amusing enough; it is honest, but too pedestrianly; it is realistic, but on themes which are too tiny and too recurrent. It bears about it an *insect* quality; it fidgets the nerves and conscience to no purpose. And it is, for all its pieties, devoid of spiritual pain. It is without light and it is somehow ignoble. In fact I might easily call it a very depressing work. But history and the world are against me – and it is the most famous, the most read and perhaps the best loved of all known diaries.

It is curious that these two most famous of all English diaries remained unpublished until more than a century after the deaths of their authors, and then appeared within seven years of each other: Evelyn's – by permission of the Evelyn family, and edited by William Bray – in 1818; Pepys' in 1825, under the editorship of Lord Braybrooke. Pepys had indeed taken careful measures against easy publication. He wrote his diary in a mixture of shorthand – Shelton's system – and a misleading confusion of foreign words and invented jargon. The manuscript was among his books, which he bequeathed to Magdalene College, Cambridge – and English literature owes one of its most curious and famous possessions to the extraordinarily patient research of an undergraduate of Cambridge called John Smith, who deciphered the text between 1819 and 1822. When it was published in 1825 it naturally caused a vast sensation – and, like Evelyn's Diary, threw floods of light upon seventeenth-century society.

Men of the world, Evelyn and Pepys; and their records, though decently strewn with Christian sentiments, portray a society of worldlings, of men and women committed to personal pleasure and personal success. But parallel with their long, complacent lives lived in the glittering capital ran another – spent at first in English villages and country towns, and later either in prisons or on long, difficult journeys in Holland and Germany, in America and the West Indies; and not 'steeple-counting', as Evelyn might have said, but in pursuit of souls, in spread of grace. George Fox, a weaver's son and the first of the Quakers, was born in Leicestershire in 1624, and died in London in 1691. His *Great Journal* is little read now, I imagine – save by members of the faith he founded; and indeed for the uninitiated layman it makes uneasy, unattractive reading. It is crude, naïve and often turgid; it repeats and overstresses, and labours with too pugnacious simplicity experiences and trains of mystical thought which cannot be conveyed by so much positiveness. But it is impossible to open it anywhere and read a page or two without feeling the pure force of the man behind it, the spiritual generosity, the sheer missionary goodwill. It is the textbook of life dominated by zeal for the good, and by natural

(above) *Samuel Pepys in 1666. The music he holds is his own setting of Davenant's 'Beauty retire'. 'Music and women I cannot but give way to, whatever my business is',* wrote Pepys. (left) *The final page of Pepys's shorthand diary, abandoned in 1669 because of (unfounded) fears for his failing eyesight.*

The Quakers were organized by George Fox; this detail from a contemporary print shows them gathered for a meeting in the time of Queen Anne. Fox's Journal *rests on the table in the centre.*

understanding of goodness; it is the record of one who quite simply *applied* mysticism to daily life and was perfectly content to suffer for this peculiarity, and to go on preaching its necessity in all times and places, to his last breath. The *Journal* is an important spiritual work not because it possesses any high literary merit, but because it is passionately sincere and generous, and is the first record of the humble, difficult and often desperate beginnings of a faith which was to become a great social force, and one of the brightest, steadiest lamps which religion has ever lighted upon earth.

No collector of English diaries can escape the Woodforde family. It is probable that between 1600 and 1820 there can hardly have been a day on which one Woodforde or another did not note down what he ate for dinner or what the weather was like, or that the harvest was carried, or that the tailor overcharged him for mending a waistcoat. They were a respectable Northamptonshire and Somerset family of parsons, soldiers, sailors and country gentlemen – and almost all had the diary-hobby, even that one of them, the second or third Samuel Woodforde, who stepped so far out of their tradition as to become a painter, and an R.A. In 1932 a twentieth-century member of the family, Miss Dorothy Heighes Woodforde, published a volume of extracts from what appears to be a great mass of journals – which indicates that between them the Woodfordes have assembled an enormously full and detailed record of English country life over a period of about two hundred and fifty years. It seems that the diaries of Samuel the Academician are merely dull notes of commissions undertaken and people met – and I gather from references to him in Farington's *Diaries* that he was a dry stick of a man, of no particular charm or talent; but such pages as I have read from certain other members of the family have got a kind of slow, comfortable reality in them, and a gentle, unexacting variation of colour and theme, suggestive of English landscape, and carrying the conservative, traditional, place-bound quality, and if you like, charm of English country-house life. Menus, recipes, small scandals, small journeys; exchange of neighbourly courtesies and acrimonies; little kindnesses, little tasks; an earache, an inoculation; the text of a sermon, a 'scene' of some kind in church; sixpence won at cards, or a maidservant's dismissal; a snowstorm, a ripening of cucumbers, a rumour from the wars in France; the garden, the weather, the walk before dinner – always these three – the garden, the weather . . . it is England that they give us, the Woodfordes; one particular England, the one they knew and counted on and took for granted as their especial right and pleasure always. And they wrote it down, Nancy, Robert, Samuel, James, with that careful literalness, that adherence to presented facts and unconsciousness of lurking ideas, which has always been the staple of conversation in houses such as theirs, they give us English country-house life, its very accent and idiom, exactly as the English upper class has evolved and cherished it.

And one Woodforde took the family's hobby a very long way, and made it famous in his own person. The Reverend James Woodforde, born in Somerset in 1740, and Rector of Weston Longeville in Norfolk from 1776 to 1803, the year of his death, began his diary when he was eighteen and kept it up faithfully for the remaining forty-five years of his natural span. *The Diary of A Country Parson*, published in five volumes by the

Nancy Woodforde, one of the most indefatigable journal-keepers of a family of enthusiastic diarists: a chalk drawing by her relative, the painter (and diarist) Samuel Woodforde.

Oxford University Press, became celebrated at its first bow, and is nowadays known and loved by very many readers. 'Reading the Diary of the Reverend James Woodforde is like embarking on a long voyage down a very tranquil stream', says his editor, Mr J. B. Beresford. 'There is no grand or exciting scenery; there are no rapids, *nor is there any ultimate expectation of the sea.*' The italics are mine. The five volumes are quite unbeatably non-expectant; they present as steadily as possible the obvious comings and goings, worries, kindnesses and duties, family and social obligations and pleasures of a typical unpretentious and respectable parson. Nothing more; but all is set down with a faithful intimacy, and with that repetitiveness which is unavoidable in so close and long a record – so that reading of life in the Weston parsonage – first with troublesome nephew Bill for second string, and later with diary-keeping niece Nancy – becomes after a volume or so the same thing as living there. And it is not altogether dull. There are touches of scandal and fuss; there are parties – an astonishingly catastrophic one on September 16th, 1777; there is a great deal of food and drink; there are the excitements of the rhubarb purge: 'Sister Clarke, Nancy, Sam and myself all took it into our heads to take a good dose of Rhubarb going to bed . . .'; and there are outbreaks of horseplay. 'Mrs Davie and Nancy made me up an Apple Pye Bed last night.' 'I took Mrs Davie's garter to-night and kept it. I gave her my pair of garters and I am to have her other to-morrow.' The parson was over forty at this time. 'There are green fields on either side', says Mr Beresford, in further description of this diary, 'and trees, and a very pleasant murmuring of water . . .'. True enough. It catches all the quiet of its place; it is a benevolent, placid record of habits and customs, unruffled by any hint of mind, or of a private life in the breast.

The Reverend William Cole, of Blechely, Waterbeach and Milton Parsonages, was less suave of temperament that Mr Woodforde; indeed malicious, contentious, eccentric and with a fair span of tastes and interests – as might be expected of a friend and correspondent of Horace Walpole. His life ran from 1714 to 1782; but his diaries, as they have been given to us by Constable, edited by Mr F. G. Stokes and introduced by Miss Helen Waddell, cover only the years 1765 to 1770, when he was in his earlier fifties. The first of these diaries deals with a sojourn in Paris in 1765, whilst Walpole was living there; the remainder are of country parsonage life, and thick with detail of characters, happenings and humours – to say nothing of details of farm and garden, of food and drink, of health, domestic managements and the expenditure of money. All sharply seasoned with the Reverend William's authoritativeness, guile and acrimony, as well as some pungent reflections on Church and general affairs. He was a meticulous, fussy bachelor, very domesticated and with individual taste. He packs his journals with all these interests, and although the details are wearisome, and there are too many names, too many small disputes, too many capital letters, and too much eccentricity in his prose style, for some tastes – he is undoubtedly an oddity, and has left himself and his scene alive and rich and contributory behind him, for the occasional pleasure of the curious and the nostalgic.

And while the unhurried lives of these divines plodded forward – 'wrote . . . to send a porter to Mr Walpole's for my French china and Pastilles which he bought for me at Paris', says Mr Cole; and 'A very comical dull day with us all. Sister Clarke very low. In the evening Sam spoke in favour of the Methodists, rather too much I think', says Mr Woodforde –

Methodism, having long flooded out from Oxford's Holy Club and 'our little society in Fetter Lane', was sweeping up and down the island, preaching the grace of God without pause or compromise and indeed by 1770 having established 'The Lord our Righteousness' – newly, formidably, as an uncrushable social force – in Scotland, in Ireland and in New England. John Wesley, born in a Lincolnshire rectory in 1703, had taken Holy Orders and been made a fellow of Lincoln College, Oxford before Rev. James Woodforde was born, and while Mr Cole was still at Eton; and as he wasted no time in developing and exercising his missionary vocation, before the latter were middle-aged men the Methodist societies and meetings were a constant part of English life and English news – a controversy, an anxiety, but beyond question a passionate, true force, from which the respect of honest men could not be withheld, and which was impervious to the malignancies of prejudice. And if anyone wonders why a simple, scriptural apostolate, an unblushing appeal to goodness and the sources of grace, could so effectively and rapidly disturb alike the lazy privilege, the sceptic rationalism and the dark, lost ignorance of eighteenth-century England, he has only to acquaint himself even a little, by a volume or so of his writing, with John Wesley. And the easiest and truest way to do this is to read a part, or the whole, of his great *Journal*.

We find there all the chief things that this remarkable man was: the energy, the passion, the organizing power, the foresight, the adaptability, the courage and the trenchant, economical eloquence – all of which had share in his missionary success. As a record of sheer, unbroken industry alone it defeats most known biographies, and it paints a very remarkable portrait of a man complicated by a great endowment of attributes – emotional, hard-headed, domineering, intellectual, even sceptical, and brave; a conservative reformer, a reactionary radical, an arrogant, self-confident saint – all co-ordinated by singleness of purpose, so that a very human man becomes a supernatural force, to transform the lives and hearts of millions.

The story the *Journal* tells is enormous; because it is businesslike and thorough and covers the oft-repeated labour of sixty years, it is sometimes dull country for the modern reader, and sometimes, since we cannot merely by reading of this extraordinary apostolate, find Wesley's 'peace with God', we can only read in astonished acceptance the scripturally phrased descriptions of conversion. 'Then God began to make bare his arm in an extraordinary manner. Those who were strangers to God felt as

Wesley preaching in the amphitheatre near Gwennap, Cornwall: a print by W. O. Geller. Wesley's Journal *records: 'We reached Gwennap . . . and found the plain covered from end to end. It was supposed there were 10,000 people.'*

it were a sword in their bones, constraining them to roar aloud.' Nor can we feel at ease, at our remove from the fresh impulse, when we read of little children that 'sometimes one, sometimes more, prayed aloud; sometimes a cry went up from them all, till five or six of them, who were in doubts before, saw the light of God's countenance'. But perhaps we can a little measure what we do not understand or feel at home with in Wesley's *Journal* by those parts of it that we can apprehend: the honesty, the courage, the mercy and the sheer love of men that bind it together; the trenchancy of the unaffected prose; the intelligence of the diarist's comments on his very catholic reading – and, above all, the generous bitterness, the truth, shrewdness and mercy of his observation of life as he finds it: 'Our eyes and ears may convince us there is not a less happy body of men in all England than the country farmers. In general their life is

*Edward Gibbon. A silhouette made in 1791,
when the historian and diarist was living in Lausanne, after the completion
of his history of the decline of the Roman Empire.*

supremely dull, and it is usually unhappy too.' There is plenty of such non-sentimental comment all through the volumes; highly disturbing to the lazy and the comfortable – as John Wesley compelled his Methodism to be.

Two intellectuals of the eighteenth century wrote diaries which are alike in that each reveals an aspect of its writer's temperament which the rest of his life either concealed or hardly suggests to us. In 1761, when Edward Gibbon was twenty-four and serving as a Captain in the South Hampshire Militia he began a diary, which he kept with fair regularity during three years. The latter part of it, from his arrival in Paris in January 1763 until he reached Rome in May 1764 – when it ceased – is written in French. It is not a very full, deep or elaborate journal, but it gives an interesting account of his reading and the directions of his thought at a time when he had not yet made up his mind about future work; also it throws some light on the difficulties placed in the way of a temperament such as Gibbon's – scholarly, ironic, non-combative and of indifferent physical health – by the affectionate interference and domination of an ambitious father, whose only child he was; and chiefly it is entertaining in that it offers us an unexpected picture – amusing, tolerant and altogether to his credit – of the historian of the Roman Empire in training as a British soldier. As one reads of the scrupulous pains he took with his duties, of how loyally he cared for the prestige and the comfort of his men, of how honestly he gave his attention to the incongruous life – with only a very occasional mild grumble, 'tired of companions who had neither the knowledge of scholars nor the manners of gentlemen' – one is reminded of many young men of his mental colour, who are to-day in like case with Gibbon, though risking much more than he was asked to risk; not geniuses all, indeed, though one among them may be – but like him impressively gracious and scrupulous in accepting a distasteful occupation and adapting themselves to it. 'I exercised the Battalion for the fourth time, officers and eighteen rounds. These field days were of some service both to men and officers. I am sure they were of the greatest to me.' 'We had a field day . . . Tho' I had not exercised them so long yet I found myself very clear and I believe I made no mistakes.' Horace Walpole might lead the wits in scepticism about these volunteers, in a vein which our Home Guard has nowadays learnt to take at its traditional worth: 'John in the rear will be firing his piece into the Backside of his friend Tom in the Front . . .' and the young man, Edward Gibbon, could be humorous too, though more subtly, about his own and his neighbours' soldiering – but while he was at it – mud, route-marches, drinking, noise, regimental disputes and all – he gave it a dutiful, even a genial attention. And leaving it, summing up the pros and cons of the experience, he says: 'But what I value most is the knowledge it has given me of mankind in general, and of my own country in particular . . . the sum of all is that I am glad the Militia has been, and glad that it is no more.'

William Windham was so versatile, so extravagantly endowed – in birth, possessions, education and friends as well as in personal abilities and graces – that it is surprising to find his career stop short of total success, but perhaps not so suprising that his diaries reveal him as a restless, unhappy man, distrustful of himself, constantly perplexed and at a loss. Yet in his lifetime the world does not seem to have been allowed to know the latter side of the medal; for when the diaries were published in 1866 – more than fifty years after his death – Lord Rosebery observed of them that they dealt 'an almost mortal blow to his reputation'. A comment difficult to understand. Surely when a man has all the gifts, such total absence of smugness as made Windham unhappy and unstable may be allowed to be, though difficult, the ultimate grace?

He was born in 1750, heir of a distinguished Norfolk name and estate. In youth at Eton and Oxford he excelled in everything, only too easily. In politics he began as a Whig, *protégé* of Fox, and spent a few months in Ireland as Secretary to the Lord Lieutenant in 1783. In 1787 he was, with Burke and Sheridan, a manager of the impeachment of Warren Hastings. At the outbreak of the French Revolution he followed Pitt, and was Secretary for War in 1794, holding office until 1801. He returned to the War Office in 1806, in the 'Ministry of All The Talents'. He died, aged sixty, in 1810. His versatility made friends for him everywhere – among Cabinet Ministers, Oxford dons, actresses, race-horse owners and women of fashion. He read Greek like a scholar, and was exceptionally endowed for mathematical studies; he loved prize-fights; he made a perilous ascent in a balloon; he interested himself in country matters and the business of his estate; he was a constant student of Shakespeare, and a close friend and critic of Mrs Siddons; he was devoted to Burke and admired by Fanny Burney; he loved Dr Johnson with devotion. He was successful with women, and – the diaries make it clear – he found the exactions of sexual love a major cause of restlessness and dissatisfaction. He had love-affairs, but the most constant and uneasy was with Mrs Byng, wife of the Hon. John Byng, afterwards Viscount Torrington. After many years of restless, uncertain intrigue with her, their feeling resolved into friendship, and late in life he married her younger sister, Cecilia Forrest, who had long been devoted to him. The marriage was childless, and appears to have been happy.

The journals make dry and somewhat tired comment on all the emotions, friendships, ambitions, projects and disappointments of a full life. They are revelatory only of Windham's dissatisfaction with himself, and into that they do not plunge wholeheartedly. They ring wearily for the most part; there is nothing in them to resolve the enigma of his life, or expose its heart – but they do deepen and underline it, adding a grace of sadness and second thoughts to a personal history which might otherwise seem monotonously brilliant.

We will depart from the eighteenth century under the nimble, bright escort of Fanny Burney. She breaks new ground. For one thing, she is the

William Windham, painted by Joshua Reynolds in 1788. His diary reveals the self-doubts and hypochondria which beset his successful political career.

first English *woman* of any significance – *pace* the Woodforde ladies – who has left us a diary. For another, she leads us, a little unfairly, towards a suspicion which later increases somewhat, that women make more refreshing, more effective diarists than men. Be that as it may, you may have your Pepys and Evelyn and, with both hands, the pettifogging parsons – except Rev. Francis Kilvert – if you will leave me Fanny Burney; all the uneven, over-written seventy years of her industrious and spirited jotting-down.

She was born in 1752 and she died in 1840; she began to keep her diary in 1768, when she was sixteen, and she made her last entry in it on 5th March 1839, when she was eighty-seven. 'I broke off, and an incapable unwillingness seized my pen', that last note begins – and we feel the old lady's petulant surprise. Incapable unwillingness had not normally been her trouble with a pen. Indeed her *Juvenile Journal*, covering the years before she published *Evelina* and 'Addressed to a Certain Miss Nobody' is torrentially, excessively facile – and at times too facetious and coy for present-day taste. But when she romps overmuch, we can remind ourselves that she is very young, at least during the first four or five hundred pages, and also that a great deal of the clatter is in fact sheer talent that has not yet perceived or taken hold of itself. And perhaps the final impression left with us when we reach 5th March 1839 is that – for all her success, for all the brilliance and fun and fame, and though she will always hold a place in English letters – the gifted creature never measured her own powers, never extended or wrestled with them, and thus never became the writer she was born to be. Her first success surprised and enchanted her – and she seems to have gone on being surprised, enchanted and a touch amateurish to the end.

Most people know the outline of her life. She was one of the large family of Dr Charles Burney, musician and historian of music, and she spent a free and happy girlhood in London, educating herself at random and enjoying the brilliant, varied society of her father's friends – musical, theatrical, intellectual and merely fashionable. She surprised her world and her family, with *Evelina* when she was twenty-six, becoming famous at a blow, and becoming moreover Dr Johnson's 'Fannikin' and his 'little Burney'. Reynolds, Burke, Windham, Sheridan became her friends; Mrs Thrale took her up, and she met Mrs Montague and all the 'Blues'; Madame de Genlis sought her out on her first visit to England, and wooed her friendship; and the aged Mrs Delany patronized her – with the unfortunate result that the foolish Fanny, after having repeated the *Evelina* success with *Cecilia*, found herself, at the age of thirty-three and when a famous woman of letters, installed as Second Mistress of the Robes to Queen Charlotte, the dull wife of George III. 'And now began a slavery of five years', says Macaulay, and '. . . we are utterly at a loss to conceive how any human being could endure such a life, while there remained a vacant garret in Grub Street, a crossing in want of a sweeper, a parish workhouse or a parish vault'. Without being quite so extravagantly at a loss, we marvel too – especially as we read the diarist's brilliantly revelatory account of life as Queen Charlotte's attendant. It was an absurd appointment, and it broke Miss Burney's health and she had to be released from it. Thereafter she fell into the society of some *émigrés* from the French Revolution and in 1793, at the age of forty-one, she married the penniless Chevalier d'Arblay and settled down with him in a cottage in Surrey, to live on her court pension of £100 a year. They had one child, a son, and they were very happy. The diaries are in nothing better than in their restrained, true portrayal of her marital peace, and the sweetness and gaiety with which they recount the baby years of her child, and her delight in him. From 1801 to 1810 she lived in France, her husband's fortunes being somewhat restored under Napoleon; she brought her son back to England in the latter year, and rejoined her husband in France in 1814. She was in Brussels in 1815, and her diaries contain a famous account of June of that year, and the thunders and repercussions of Waterloo. Thereafter her husband settled in England again, until his death in 1818. Her son, who became a clergyman, died unmarried in 1837. Between her marriage and her death she did much literary work – some unsuccessful plays, a novel, *Camilla*, and an unreadable novel called *The Wanderer*, for which she is said to have received £7,000; also *Memoirs of Dr Burney* and some pamphlets – as well as the never neglected diaries.

It is well she did not neglect them, for they are the best of her, and her chief claim on immortality. They are so much better than most diaries because they are imaginative, free and subjective; they are, in fact, the work of a *writer*, which most diaries are not. Miss Burney does not stick to the facts of each day in the sense of merely setting them down; she uses them, expands them, enjoys herself with them, and lets us take all those details for granted which she does not select as essential to her vein of narrative. She gives us conversations – with Mrs Thrale, with Windham, with George III, with Talleyrand, or with her little son – not *verbatim* or in any kind of shorthand but as her imagination and her brilliant memory feel them when they echo in her afterwards – so that they are truer than truth and, without strain or apparent falsification, achieve a richness, a certainty of character and a sequence and pace which in fact they almost certainly did not have, but which the artist rightly felt they merited.

As we read, and taste the variety of her experiences and the power, understanding and charm which she brought to bear on all she encountered, we cannot but wonder why she never took herself in hand and became a great novelist, as great as Jane Austen. She seems to have had all the needed natural abilities; and she had besides a wide knowledge of life and the world, she had the goodwill of all the best minds of her day, she had health and long life and a great zest for writing. Yet she never mastered these advantages and soared to genius on them.

The reason may lie with her benevolent and rather foolish father. Not in any of his conscious acts – for though it clearly was silly of him to persuade her, with Mrs Delany, into becoming a Mistress of the Robes, we do not go all the way with Macaulay in his shocked tirades against the Doctor for this ill-judged piece of snobbery and worldly hopefulness – for Fanny was, after all, thirty-one then and famous, and had twice resoundingly proved her ability to succeed in letters; she could have decided for herself against an undertaking which, the diaries make clear, she viewed with uneasy fear. 'I have always and uniformly had a horror of a life of attendance and dependence . . . Could I but save myself from a lasting bond?' However, she did not save herself; and this major occasion is only the full declaration of a curious docility that ran all through her life, often weakening or tarnishing its merits.

I trace this to her father – and not to any fault of his, but to his unconscious, potent influence on her. She loved him very much, and he was in childhood and girlhood the source and inspirer of all that ease and fun and pleasant learning and talented go-as-you-please in which she and her sisters were so happy. The love, the confidence he bred in Fanny would seem to have trained her into a marked dependence on the elderly, and a curious need to be loved by them, and to take their directions. She loved her father; and also in girlhood she loved the elderly Mr Samuel Crisp of Chessington. 'Daddy' Crisp, for whom with her sister Susan all

(above) *Fanny Burney, novelist and energetic diarist, painted by E. Burney.* (left) *The royal family promenades on the terrace at Windsor, George III and Queen Charlotte bringing up the rear. Fanny Burney abandoned literary life in London to take up the post of Second Mistress of the Robes to the queen; her diary gives a vivid account of her exhausting life at the court of a frequently deranged king.*

the early diaries were written. 'My papa always mentions him by the name of my *Flame*. Indeed he is not mistaken – himself is the only man on earth I prefer to him.' She loved Dr Johnson with veneration for the last years of his life, and sought his company constantly, though she was only in her twenties; she was for a time during Dr Johnson's life the slave of the already elderly Mrs Thrale; she adored the venerable and boring Mrs Delany; she persuaded herself that she adored the 'sweet Queen' Charlotte, and similarly that she had a great affection for poor George III at his maddest and feeblest; and when at last she loved a man enough to marry him, he too was elderly, in his middle fifties. All these people, from elderly to aged, were at different periods the dominating influences in her life; they advised her, they moulded her, and she seemingly found it impossible ever to doubt their wisdom, be sceptical about them, or give them, however privately, a disrespectful or a rebellious thought. They intimidated her, though she did not perceive it, for she needed, in some obscure way, their elderly authority; she needed, in every important relationship, to find an element of her first strong filial devotion. And all these influences, while they made her happy and flattered her and gave her a sense of safety, not only led her away from her more forceful and self-reliant parts, in which she might have found the true ore of her talent, but also turned her back from adventures in friendship which might have helped her to that end. For constantly in the diaries we are disappointed by fits of prudery and caution which can only have been induced by the shocked gossip of the old, and must have arisen from the docile need to 'please papa' in everything – as when she nonsensically took Dr Johnson's cue and ended her friendship with Mrs Thrale because the latter chose to marry Mr Piozzi; and later in life abandoned in turn her friends Madame de Genlis and Madame de Staël – simply because of *rumours* about their private lives and while protesting her personal sense of loss and her admiration of the ladies' talents. Such parochialism and docility to the views of the cautious sit ill with her wit, her keen interest in character and her general liveliness and *verve*. But they run all through the bright fibre of her life, and seem to spring from that early, first desire to be everything her father most admired. All the rest of life had to be dovetailed into that essential.

'November 11th, Wednesday. Baked bread and giblet pie—put books in order—mended stockings. Put aside dearest C.'s letters, and now at about

Dorothy Wordsworth in 1833, aged sixty-one; her journals were a source of poetic inspiration to her brother as well as a valuable record of their everyday life together.

seven o'clock we are sitting by a nice fire. Wm. with his book and a candle, and Mary writing to Sara.' It is 1801, we are at Grasmere, and Dorothy Wordsworth is making her gentle note of the day. And it is hardly necessary for us to interrupt her, or do more than name her here among our English diarists – for the publication in 1941 of all her *Journals*, under the editorship of Mr E. de Selincourt, created such a happy new *réclame* for her and was received with such universal pleasure that she certainly stands in no further need of commendation. And I observe this all the more contentedly since I have to admit – making, so far as I know, a minority of one – that the *Journals* disappoint me taken as a whole, and when considered in relation to the personality we know their writer to have been. All except the *Grasmere Journal* (1800–3) and the brief *Alfoxden Journal*, which in their kind – though not the kind we might have longed for – are perfect; and parts of the *Journal Of A Tour In The Isle Of Man* (1828), which in spite of premonitory shadows here and there of sadness and ill-health contains much of the simple, lyrically-touched realism, the fastidious, clear selectiveness which distinguish so especially the Grasmere pages.

But though we could not spare any one of her exquisitely measured strokes of simple observation – 'Wytheburn looked very wintry, but yet there was a foxglove blossoming by the roadside—' knowing Dorothy Wordsworth somewhat from the loves and friendships she won and kept – from Coleridge, from the Lambs, from Crabb Robinson, from all her brother's admirers, and from the adored brother himself – we want from her in her writings more of that 'meddling intellect' that William inveighed against; we want her thoughts as well as her observations, and when she 'walked with Coleridge', when 'William and I strolled in the wood', when 'we had a sweet and tender conversation' we desire exasperatedly to know a little at least of what was said. There is too much suppression everywhere in Dorothy Wordsworth of what clearly must have been a most distinguished and original mind; too much daily practice of that 'wise passiveness' which William invoked, but – we surmise, for all his sister's passionate care of his legend – did not easily command. Curiously, we might think after reading her *Journals* that Dorothy is, by temperament, that ideal poet of the Preface to *Lyrical Ballads* whom William believed himself to be. But she did not write verse, and she undertook to be William's angel – so egoism and intellectual restlessness were subjugated by responsibility and by love; and she is so loyal, so discreet that we are never allowed to guess at any possible second thoughts. Her glinting, delicate sense of humour, which she uses sparingly, is never allowed to hurt William or anyone else – although his humourlessness, his quality of seeming to have been born an old man, must often have puzzled, not to say wearied, a companion so girlishly, though fastidiously, willing to be amused. The poet was, when he travelled abroad, prone to make scenes – and though Dorothy records these as justified, she cannot quite keep humorous uneasiness at bay. 'Mary and I walked on ahead . . .' and 'Wm. refused to give more than the sum agreed for—the man grew impertinent—and William desired the Magistrate might be summoned—a woful resource!' Such gleams relieve the repetitive descriptions of scenery which abound in *A Tour Of The Continent* (1820); but there are not enough of them, and there is far too much guide-book observation. Love made her too discreet. No one could wish her to be crudely expansive about, for instance, the trip she took with William to Calais in August 1802, to visit Annette and his daughter Caroline, before his marriage to Mary Hutchinson – but is it unnatural to be surprised that the curcumstances induced no greater depth of comment, no closer or more individual reflections than she made on any other of their journeys?

Still, she has left us the small, imperishable beauties of the *Grasmere Journal*, its constant loveliness heightened by numerous sweet, plain touches. '. . . I sate half an hour afraid to pass a cow. The cow looked at me and I looked at the cow, and whenever I stirred the cow gave over eating.' 'The Lake of Rydale calm, Jupiter behind, Jupiter at least *we* call him, but William says we always call the largest star Jupiter.' '. . . at last I eased my heart by weeping—nervous blubbering, says William. It is not so.'

Between 1809 and 1811 an eccentric poor governess lived at a house called Dove's Nest on Windermere. 'There are many characters here worth observation', she wrote in her diary, or letter-book. 'S. Coleridge, the conductor of a new and valued publication entitled "The Friend," resides only a few miles hence.' But she never mentions the Wordsworths, with whom Coleridge was then living at Allan Bank; and though she occasionally records going to Grasmere church on Sunday she does not seem to have known that a great poet lived so near her. Her employers, the wild and frantic Pedders who led her a terrible dance, would not have been sympathetic to William or to 'dearest C.' – so the remarkable and forthright Miss Weeton, brushing just wide of a chance of mention in Miss Wordsworth's diaries, did well, and rather better, to keep her own.

She was an obscure, unlucky woman, born in Upholland, Lancashire, in 1777, and brought up in great poverty by her widowed mother who kept a little dame school, and handed it on to her daughter. Miss Weeton forged out from it in exasperation in her thirties and became a governess, scraped an independent living one way and another, was trapped by a brother, for his own ends, into a wretched marriage, stormed out of that, fought a long, wild battle for the custody of her one child – won the battle, established herself as a respectable citizen in Wigan, and died feared, and long remembered I should think by all her relatives and connections. The humble but vehement and unusual story was set down by her, year in year out, in vigorous diaries, and in letters which she copied and embodied very carefully in the diaries. These were neglected and ignored by her people after her death, but by chance in the '30s of this century fell into the sympathetic hands of Mr Edward Hall and, edited by him, were published by the Oxford University Press in two volumes, in 1936 and 1939. They run from 1807 to 1825, and give a close, realistic picture of small-town life in England at that time – while building up with amazing strokes of humour, coarseness, truth, self-acclamation, pride and intelligence, a full-size portrait of a very remarkable female – one who in an easier walk of life, or with even an ounce or two more of education or of luck, might have done remarkable things, or given a lot of trouble, or somehow made herself remembered. Space forbids me to linger with Miss Weeton – I can only commend her in passing to those who like originals, and do not mind being bludgeoned – at a remove of more than a hundred years.

In the great world at this period, far from the Lakes and from Upholland – in Fanny Burney's world – a great many journals were piling up, in secret or in semi-secret. The first half of the nineteenth century saw well to its own documentation. Creevey, Greville, Croker; Joseph Farington, Benjamin Haydon; Lady Blessington, Lady Holland; Moore, Byron, Rogers, Telford, Scott – these and many others consumed a great deal of ink in their day, assembling what were to be their 'papers' – memoirs, reminiscences, letters – not always diaries. Thomas Creevey, for instance, who moved in Prince Regent and Holland House circles, was believed by Greville and others to have kept 'copious diaries', as to the destiny of which there was some anxiety at his death in 1838. But when his 'papers' were published there was found to be almost no diary – only an occasional passage in that form wedged in among his letters to his wife and to his stepdaughter. These letters are, however, so lively and malicious that one cannot but regret the diaries of which he was suspected, but which perhaps he never wrote.

Charles Greville, who held the post of Clerk to the Council and was intimate with statesmen of all parties, and particularly with the Duke of Wellington and with Palmerston, kept journals from 1818 to 1860, had a wonderful *flair* for the right kind of backstairs news, and has provided posterity with some excellent entertainment. Joseph Farington R.A., an

Benjamin Haydon in 1816: a self-portrait. Haydon would despair to know that he is to-day remembered for his journal and his friendship with Keats rather than for his painting.

inconsiderable painter, but a man of authority and shrewdness who devoted himself zestfully to Academy affairs, kept a diary from 1793 to the last day of his life, December 30th, 1821. Everyone who is anyone appears in it, and therefore it is a useful reference book for historians or biographers of the period; but in manner and tone it is dull, and does nothing to attract us to its writer.

A very different kind of man, Benjamin Haydon – resembling Farington only in being a bad painter – also kept a journal, from 1821 to his death, by suicide, in 1846. Haydon was energetic, pugnacious, intelligent, most naïvely conceited and never out of trouble – and his diary reflects him vividly, and is alternately maddening and very entertaining.

Henry Crabb Robinson, drawn by J. J. Masquerier.
Robinson commented on this drawing in his diary: 'My very best expression.
It need be the best to be endurable.'

He has a good narrative manner and plenty of humour, except about himself, a subject on which he could not look unemotionally. He makes good observations on painters: 'Tintoretto has not the solidity of Rubens or Titian; Titian was full of sensation.' And he reports parties well – the terrible christening party for Hazlitt's child, and an evening when Mrs Siddons read *Macbeth* to a number of gentlemen who were eating toast and drinking tea, they in an agony lest they clatter or crunch. 'Curious to see Lawrence in that predicament, to hear him bite by degrees and then stop for fear of making too much crackle.' Haydon was a friend and correspondent of Keats, of whom he says with absurd complacency:

'Poor, dear Keats. Had Nature but given you firmness as well as fineness of nerve . . .'. Yet, years after Keats' death, he writes touchingly: 'I dreamt last night of dear Keats. I thought he appeared to me and said: "Haydon you promised to make a drawing of my head". . .'. Haydon died in sudden despair, after years blustering for solvency and fame – and he is remembered now not as a painter, not even as the man who fought the Academy in the cause of the Elgin Marbles, but merely as a friend of Keats, and perhaps also because Hazlitt said he was the best talker he ever knew.

But the period of all these journals, indeed the first sixty years of the nineteenth century, have been recorded quite superbly – from the point of view of historians, biographers and gossip-hunters – by a prince of extrovert diarists, Henry Crabb Robinson. What we have in published form of this indefatigable man – reminiscences, letters and diaries – and a very great deal has not been printed – makes an invaluable body of information and eye-witness comment. To try to catalogue Crabb Robinson's famous friends, or his interests, or his travels, or his social activities would be absurd. He had, since he must have been abnormally sociable, a wonderful life. He was of respectable, modest origin, the son of a tanner in Bury St Edmunds. He spent his youth as an attorney's clerk; then, inheriting an income of £100 a year, he went to Germany when he was twenty-five, and remained there five years, studying at Jena and Frankfurt, and later meeting in Weimar all the greatest Germans of the century – Goethe, Schiller, Wieland, Herder, Schlegel. Also he met the ubiquitous Madame de Staël, and 'mon Benjamin', Benjamin Constant. In England, to which he returned in 1805, his earliest friends – but he never seemed to lose a friend or to slacken in the upkeep of friendship – were Hazlitt, the Lambs, Mrs Barbauld, Coleridge, the Wordsworths, the Flaxmans, Blake, Miss Mitford – but eventually every interesting, intelligent or especially gifted person in England was on his list, never to be removed from it. He joined the staff of *The Times* and was its correspondent in Sweden and in Spain in 1807–8. From 1813 to 1838 he practised at the Bar and having made enough money with which to be solvent and generous for the rest of his days he retired, to give himself up to a variety of good works and pleasant pursuits.

He was not a brilliant man; but he had a sound understanding, was industrious, loyal and balanced, and he must have had a genius for friendship. His diaries are innocent of malice, but they are not at all fatuous. His sturdy devotion to Coleridge through thick and thin, his unflurried interest in Blake, and his wise, calm passion – if passion *can* be thus qualified – for Goethe prove capacity of mind and an appetite for the difficult. And the value for us of his devotion to genius is the simplicity, unaffected and pure of sycophancy, with which he writes down his impressions, When he notes some of Blake's difficult aphorisms: 'I regret that I have been unable to do more than put down these few things', he says. 'The tone and manner are incommunicable. There are a natural sweetness and gentility about Blake which are delightful.'

The modest diarist might have been surprised to learn that *his* readers in their turn would find, all through his laborious contributions to posterity another kind of 'natural sweetness and gentility . . . which are delightful'.

Crabb Robinson does not appear to have known Caroline Fox, although many of his friends were also hers, and he would have sympathized with her intellectual interests and with her spiritual idiom. She kept a diary, from 1835, when she was sixteen, to her death in 1871. She was born and always made her home in Cornwall. Her father was Robert Were Fox, Quaker, distinguished geologist and F.R.S. Caroline, who never married, was herself a devout Quaker, and of intellectual and austere tastes – though warm and humorous too, very quick and appreciative with life and people. Chief among her famous friends were John Stuart Mill, John Sterling and the Carlyles. She regularly paid long visits to London, and went abroad with her father on his travels and, towards the end of her life, in search of health. Her *Journal*, though in fact a touch too impersonal for all its air of ease and intimacy, is a very intelligent record of the observations and moods of many great and distinguished people; there are attractive notes on the diarist's own reading, and there is a sense of sweetness and natural holiness throughout. Good anecdotes too: Jane Welsh Carlyle reporting of Geraldine Jewsbury that she 'declares herself born without any sense of decency; the publishers beg that she will be decent, and she has not the slightest objection to be so, but she does not know what it is'. Sir Henry de la Beche and Warington Smyth being unnerved at a dinner party by the young Florence Nightingale, who led them *via* geology 'into regions of Latin and Greek' and Egyptian inscriptions. 'But when she began quoting Lepidus . . . "A capital young lady that, if she hadn't so floored me with her Latin and Greek!" ' Tennyson, in 1860: '. . . but when he heard the name of Hallam, how his great grey eyes opened, and gave one a momentary glimpse of the depths in which *In Memoriam* learnt its infinite wail'.

In 1938, '39, '40 there appeared for the first time in print – published by Jonathan Cape – three volumes entitled *Kilvert's Diary*. Mr William Plomer was their editor. He had found a prize indeed – and the prize fell luckily into discreet and sympathetic hands. Anything might have happened to Francis Kilvert when being dressed for presentation to the reading public of the past twenty years, for he lays his soul right open to the mockery, the cleverness of the portentous psycho-analytical wisdom of our time. Mr Plomer, however, was content to read and enjoy him, assemble all available facts and associations, and present the diarist to us with only the necessary amount of just and friendly comment.

Francis Kilvert was born in a Somerset rectory in 1840. He went to Oxford and took Holy Orders. After a period assisting his father, who was then rector of Langley Burrell in Wiltshire, he went as curate to Clyro in Radnorshire, where he worked for seven years. Afterwards he had a living at St Harmon's in Radnorshire, and finally that of Bredwardine in Herefordshire. He married when he was thirty-eight, and five weeks after his marriage he died very suddenly of peritonitis. His published diary runs, with breaks, from 1870 to the spring of the year in which he died, 1879.

Its most obvious merit is the clear and detailed picture it gives us of life in the English countryside seventy years ago. Kilvert gets it all in, and makes it much more vivid and worth reading about than do the eighteenth-century parsons, because he has enthusiasm for living, takes pains, has an unusually eager, bright eye, and – being very sentimental – gets all external things related to himself. He gives us, like a painter, not the flat actuality but his own composition of it. He gives us all the 'properties' of his kind of life indeed, all the things we know that are almost 'stock' now, and that we have encountered over and over again in period novels and family albums, but he gives them *as he feels them*, and as partaking of his vitality: walks, sermons, frosty mornings, visits to parishioners; toothache, confirmation caps, talk of the Franco-Prussian War, 'a letter from my mother': girls and kisses and 'mischievous, saucy glances from beautiful grey eyes' – a very great deal about girls and glances; croquet parties, chubby babies, news from India, the funeral of an eccentric aunt (this last being quite superbly done); archery, dances, kisses – 'ten miles for a kiss'; prayers by the bedside of dying children; a great deal of scenery; visits to Oxford; pious reflections, sudden 'romps' (undefined) – 'a screaming romp with Lucretia who in rolling about upon the bed upset the candle on the coverlet and burst into peals of

(above) *The village church of Bredwardine, Hereford and Worcester. Kilvert was vicar here from 1877 until his death in 1879. He is buried in the churchyard.*

(right) *Verses and drawings by Francis Kilvert, recalling a nutting expedition to Seagry Woods on Saturday 4 September, 1875. Kilvert himself leans against the gate in the top drawing: 'We had a grand scramble and merry romp . . . racing up and down the green rides, clambering over the high gates gathering nuts, throwing burrs at each other and sticking them in the girls' hair amidst shouts and screams of laughter . . .'.*

inextinguishable laughter . . .'; talks with Mr Barton, 'a clever, well-read man', about the Holy Grail; 'sun on the lawn . . . claret cup iced . . . after dinner we had archery'. It might be dull, it might grow tiresome – even though on plain, objective merits many passages are lovely – crystal clear and complete. 'Chippenham bells pealing and firing all day for the Queen's birthday. Perch fished while I lay on the sloping bank and read *The Spanish Student*. The river was very low and the roach and dace have not yet come up. The air was full of "green drake" or mayfly just come up and all swarming over the river, and the little bleak leaping at them every this comes of having brothers —

(Edith) — "What is that scream and shout?" —

(Mabel) — "There's Evelyn's getting out."

(Tilly) — " Oh — what jolly lark

Please don't go home till it's dark" —

(Agnes) — "For Mother we must wait

Let's sit upon this gate"

'We sit upon the gate and the Battle of the Burrs again rages fiercely.'

(Edith) — " A carriage comes this way"

(Agnes) — "Whoever is it I say"

(Mabel) — "They're going a terrible pace"

(Evelyn) — "And the horse has a long white face" —

(Edith) — "I declare it's Aunt Marianne

And the chestnut horse Catch as catch can"

'a cavalcade approaches from Scagy Kienge Escorted by A.H. on foot
Inviting friends. Great crashing of boughs. laughter shouts & general uproar.'

'The Walk home — Edith running headlong down a steep green hill hand in
hand with Agnes & A.H. tumbles head over heels — & rises half stunned but laughing.'

(Edith) — " Oh — What an awful smash

My brains are all in a squash

My frock is a lively green

I declare I'm not fit to be seen"

moment.' Or this – a different statement, quite as clear and complete: 'Just as I heard the breakfast bell ring across the Common from the Rectory and turned in at the black gate a man crossed the stile carrying a basket. He said his name was Summerflower, that he had fasted since yesterday morning and that he could buy no breakfast before he had got watercresses to sell.' Yet such things, though they need not be any better done, would not in themselves bestow its curious originality and freshness on this diary. Nor would it be truthful to say that Kilvert always describes as well as in these passages. 'Considered simply as a writer of prose he shows a decided talent', says Mr Plomer. Agreed; but it is talent only – that is, talent undeveloped, unconsidered by its owner, and therefore too frequently unbridled. I am willing to be indulgent, with his editor, to his 'copious flow of adjectives' – but not for their own sakes, and not for the prose they give us when they are let loose, but because they are an unavoidable part of Francis Kilvert, they express him, for better or worse, in terms of his period and of himself – and so must be accepted with the rest of this remarkable self-portrait. But I do not think that he was more than a potential writer of good prose – for it always seems to have been hit or miss; an atmosphere, a memory, a mood could control him and make him write as it dictated; but *he* could not control those masters – which only means that he never *learnt* to write, but simply wrote; in the most alarming, rich gushes, if that was how he felt – *vide* the entry 'From My Bedroom Window' for July 11th, 1870 – or gently, objectively or humorously, when such states ruled him. I do not believe that he considered his writing at all, save with the pleasure of a boy in doing something which everyone could not do. And in the period in which he lived, with its influences of eloquence, colour, tears and tenderness, that was not a safe way to be a prose writer. Not that there is any safety – artistic or emotional – in Francis Kilvert; I think indeed that he got through so decently, as man and as writer, simply by the grace of God and the luck of the innocent.

Sometimes, taking his prose at its wildest, he reminds one of all our great-aunts, and of the poems and letters which they used to write when an infant died in the family, or had a birthday. 'Then the girls would have me go into the next room to see Janet in bed. So we went in and found her pretty and rosy with tumbled curly hair lying in her little soft white nest contentedly sucking chocolates. I sat down upon her bed and the rest gathered and so Queen Janet held her court as pleased as possible . . . soon had her round plump limbs out from under the sheets with the innocent simplicity of childhood and her pretty little feet in my lap . . . rosy and curly and still contentedly sucking her chocolate. Dear Ruthie stood by her little sister, kind, sweet and motherly. They share their little bed together, "two dumplings" as Ruthie said . . . Then the father dressed for dinner came in to see his children and to wish them Good-night. It was a lovely family group, a beautiful picture.' Or read him as he muses over a silk bookmarker with 'Forget-Me-Not' embroidered on it – 'the short, simple prayer'. 'It was a gift from a child sweetheart. But from which? I gazed at the words conscience-stricken. Forget-me-not. And I had forgotten . . . The whole scene rose before me, the old cottage fireside at evening and the fair head and pure eyes of a child bent earnestly over her work, and the little hands eager about her labour of love . . . "Forget Me Not. I will send it to-morrow and he will not forget." And I have forgotten. The vision faded. Oh, the fickleness and forgetfulness of man and the faithfulness of woman. Alas, it is the old story . . .'. It is a shame to have to chop up such a passage, but Kilvert is not economical when he dreams. And I do not quote it so much *pour rire* as to show that he wrote without judgment, though in a sense with an abundance of talent.

It is the unevenness, the eccentricity and the sheer naturalness of the writer which distinguish this diary. Kilvert puts down everything and anything, a landscape, a joke, a prayer, or a rhapsody about yet another girl; and, whatever it is, he lights it up; by some curious trick of his vitality and his innocence, he makes everything *live* that he touches.

Except perhaps girls. Because girls render him helpless. Any girl, from two years old to twenty-five, in her perambulator or at the churn or in Sunday school or being a bridesmaid or playing croquet or castrating a lamb or lying on her deathbed – any girl sets him off; about her sweet blue eyes and bright sweet morning face and rounded arms as creamy as the milk and her tossing curls and teasing glance and half-veiled charms. Girls, from their cradles to their wedding beds, moved him so much that he quite simply was unable to see them for emotion, and can be said to have been girl-blind. For it is impossible that Wiltshire, Radnorshire and Breconshire could have contained such an extraordinary number of shattering, innocent, merry beauties in that one decade seventy years ago. It is just that they were girls. 'O my child if you did but know!' and 'Ah Gipsy!' and 'Angels ever bright and fair' and 'Farewell, farewell!' and 'I thought – was it so? – that there were tears in those blue eyes when we parted.' No reader could keep track of the journey of this clergyman's heart – for apart from official wooings, of 'sweet Daisy Thomas', of 'Kathleen Mavourneen' or of 'bewitching Etty Brown', he records very,

(above) *A sketch by Queen Victoria of her taking 'tea in a snow storm' in the Cairngorms records one of the bracing outings that form such a memorable feature of her Highland Diary.*

(top) *Queen Victoria with her Indian servant, photographed in 1893 in England – despite being proclaimed Empress of India in 1876 Victoria never visited India. She kept a diary throughout her long reign (1837–1901).*

very many other strongly protested loves. 'Lovely Florence Hill' and the 'Gipsy Child' and his 'mountain maid', and the girls he 'romped' with, and the girls he longed to know better, and the little girls at Sunday school, and the girls he visited in sickness, and the girls he buried.

Parallel with this ever-rushing emotionalism runs a good rough stream of coarseness, of plain sensuality in thought, and of shameless enjoyment of the beating of children. Yet he was kind – and good. He was limited indeed by his own *naïveté* and his acceptance of outward forms, and by the characteristics, some of the worst characteristics, of his age. But he was loved in his parishes; he knew his people well, frequented them, helped them, grieved with them and 'romped' with them. He preached the Christianity of his time, and clearly he did his best to live as a Christian. He worked tirelessly and without self-pity, and in little things he was kind. If he met an old woman carrying buckets of water he carried them for her; he carried his musical box up a considerable mountain climb 'for the blind child'; in his way he understood children and made good jokes about them, and noted what they said with an unusually selective ear. And he really loved the beautiful country about him, its ancientry and simplicity, and its seasonal changes and occupations. He seems to have been a happy man on the whole in spite of his sensitivity; he had an outgoing, generous temperament, and great consideration (despite the flogging complex) for the feelings of others; he was tolerant, and touchingly easy to please. 'The morning was perfectly glorious, a brilliant cloudless blue sky . . . and the gossamers shone and twinkled into green and gold in the grass which in the shade of the wood was still hoary with the night's frost . . . After luncheon I played croquet with the girls.'

And now we will leave all this Victorianism with a salute to its Queen, who also was a diarist. Many people have read the excerpts of her diaries which are published with her letters. and many more, of the older generations, are familiar with the once very popular *Leaves From The Journal Of Our Life In The Highlands*. By reason of her place and greatness any writings of Queen Victoria must have interest, and some have found much to admire, or even to charm them, in the closer revelation of her personality which the diaries give. Some, on the other hand, have not, and remain unattracted by the dauntless, arrogant, obstinate little old lady. But certainly the Highland Diary is good fun, for us who can view those perpetual, freezing expeditions and picnics in the rain at our very safe remove. And Francis Kilvert, at least, would have admired the Queen's extraordinary prose, and shared her enthusiasm for scenery – and even perhaps for lunching 'on a cairn of stones, in a piercing cold wind'. For he was polite and adaptable in a way we have forgotten, and certainly he was a most loyal subject of Her Majesty.

So far the twentieth century has shown no sign of dropping the well-established diary habit, and we assuredly have plenty to record for those who come after. It is as well, I suppose, that the diarists should persevere. But out of the stream already published, from Sir Algernon West and Wilfrid Scawen Blunt, by way of Colonel Repington, Sir Henry Wilson and Arnold Bennett down to Ego 1, 2, 3, 4 and 5, I choose here to make reminder of only three diaries – and those reminders shall be brief. All three were written under exceptional stress and ordeal, and bear little spiritual relation to traditional English diaries – therefore they seem particularly representative of our time.

The last diary of Captain Scott is good to read now, for morale's sake, as a reminder of the power of courage, and of the dignity of men. Everyone knows the magnificent story of his last journey to the South Pole, and whoever knows the story knows the diary, which was found in the tent on the Barrier with the three dead men. The entries of the last two months are immortal. 'Wednesday January 17. – The Pole. Yes, but under very different circumstances. We have had a horrible day . . . Now for the run home and a desperate struggle. I wonder if we can do it.' 'Jan. 24th. . . . I don't like the easy way Oates and Evans get frost-bitten.' 'Feb. 8th. A lot could be written on the delight of setting foot on rock after 14 weeks of snow and ice . . . It is like going ashore after a sea voyage.' 'Feb. 24th. It is great luck having the horsemeat to add to our ration . . .'. 'Feb. 29th. Every day we have been ready to start for our depot 11 miles away but outside the door of the tent it remains a scene of whirling drift . . . we are getting weaker, of course, and the end cannot be far. It seems a pity, but I do not think I can write more. R. Scott. For God's sake look after our people.'

That was the end of one of the greatest of all stories, which can be read at any time with benefit; and now is a good time for such a cold, astringent tonic.

The Journal Of A Disappointed Man was first published in March 1919, and on its last desperate page carried the italicized announcement that Barbellion, its remarkable author, had died on December 31, 1917 – about two months after making the diary's last entry, which is the solitary word: 'Self-disgust'. Later it was found that this announcement was untrue, a

*Captain Scott writing his diary in his den at the main hut at Cape Evans of the Antarctic
expedition of 1910–13, in the course of which Scott lost his life.*

curiously ill-advised piece of 'effectiveness'; Barbellion was alive when his
Journal appeared, and died on October 22nd, 1919. This was – from the
detached point of view of readers of the *Journal* – a discouraging
discovery, and could not but chill sympathy; but the fact that he *did* live
nearly two years longer than he, we must suppose, expected to – in pain,
weakness and discomfort which it is torture to read about – was of

ultimate great value, to him and to us; for it gave him time to write *A Last Diary*, which is not nearly so well-known as the *Journal*, but which supplements and supports it – explaining, resolving much of the confused, knotted misery of the first book, and showing the disastrously unlucky man with his burden of wasted gifts and passionate regrets outgrowing, much more than the uneven courage of the *Journal* had shown him to, his terrible personal misery – and growing sweeter, lighter, truer and wittier in observation, gentler and more calm in habit of thought, as his body pressed home its violent defeat of him, and the real hour of his departure from it came in sight.

The two journals, read together, make a fine record – for they assemble *all* the essential truth about a personal tragedy which can be described as total. They take the unusually bright schoolboy – whose real name, by the way, was not Wilhelm Nero Pilate Barbellion but Bruce Frederick Cummings – with his spontaneous passion and genius for natural history from his poor and often happy days at home to the first chances, the successful examination, the post in the Natural History Museum, the stirrings of ambition, and then of love – to the premonitory encroachments of ill-health, and the beginning of a tragic, useless struggle. They give us truth about a love and a marriage, and show the goodness and necessity of that love as well as the doubts and second thoughts, not merely from the point of view of the diarist but, very justly and penetratingly, from the probable point of view of the girl who became his wife and bore him a child. They show all the theatre, all the self-pity, disgust and bewildered loneliness of a young, egoistical and brilliant man caught in a terrible trap; but also they give flashes and passages of peace, that increase and grow truer as sorrow deepens, spreading at last to an almost constant witty sweetness, a near-gaiety, in *A Last Diary*. And because of this completion, because of the clear thinking, the control, the loving-kindness and the *fun* of the end, which justify and greatly ennoble him, we can surely rejoice a little in the hard extension by two years of a life which – since by endowment he could have made it so fine – Barbellion had so ofen and so bitterly desired at an end.

He was very intelligent, in many directions. So his diaries, which exist to explain his personality and his fate to the world, as he intended them to, are not solely about himself, in the direct sense. They contain a great deal of objective observation of things and people, lively snatches of conversation, quick character-sketches and vigorous comment on books. And some of the best of these are in *A Last Diary*. His disrespectful admiration of Emily Brontë is amusingly expressed, for instance. 'One might almost write her down as Mrs Nietzsche . . . no fit companion for the young ladies of a seminary. . . . "No coward soul is mine" she tells us, with her fist held to our wincing nose.' In December 1918 he was writing: 'James Joyce is my man. Here is a writer who tells the truth about himself. It is almost impossible to tell the truth.' 'What I have always feared is coming to pass', he says, with death well in sight, 'love for my little daughter. Only another communicating string with life to be cut.' 'I take my life in homoeopathic doses now', he says gently. Somewhere he says: 'Sir Thomas Browne was my father and Marie Bashkirtseff my mother.' It is an unusually good shot. 'I am the scientific investigator of myself', he says. He was greatly gifted; and reading some of his character-impressions, and especially his conversations with his nurse towards the end, one feels that among the many things he might have done excellently the writing of novels was one.

It is curious that the last two diaries we shall speak of here, Barbellion's and Katherine Mansfield's, should be those of sick people, people doomed to die young and frustrated, and that, with Captain Scott's, their personal notes should stand for our century so far. But I cannot help the too-obvious symbolism; it has worked out that way – and need not be taken too pessimistically. For all three were brave, exceptionally brave, and all were ultimate masters of their own tragedies, though we may proportion those tragedies as we choose in relation to universal things. Katherine Mansfield's story needs no re-telling. She has left it to us in her work, in her letters, and in what she left undestroyed of her 'huge, complaining diaries'. That residue, published under the title of *Journal*, covers her life from 1914 to her death at Fontainebleau in October 1923. It is very personal, moody, self-pitying and brave. It contains notes for work, much discussion of work, sudden memories of childhood, outbursts of love, of gaiety and of desolation, and amusing, bitter, accomplished sketches of people encountered – and as it advances towards the darkness courage and ambitious desires rise up in greater waves, harder to meet, but which are met in fact by wisdom which has enlarged itself too, imperceptibly purified by detachment and humour – and by gentleness. The last pages of the *Journal* are clean of the occasional whimsicalities and false ironies that disfigure the earlier part; and there is a workmanlike, non-invalidish quality in the passages of rough notes, mere reminders for the professional – like the colour notes a painter makes. There is courage and goodness in this hard passion for work, and in the sick woman's lonely debates on the

Katherine Mansfield by her friend Anne Estelle Rice.
Her journal records life in literary London after the First World War
and her struggle against the tuberculosis which killed her.

personal question of her illness and her love. And at the end she writes, thinking of another and of how to help him: 'And when I say "I fear" don't let it disturb you, dearest heart. We all fear when we are in waiting rooms. Yet we must pass beyond them, and if the other can keep calm, it is all the help we can give each other.'

Recollecting that I began this book by saying that the best English diaries have been written by bores, I can now only hope ruefully that I have not too much justified that sweeping statement. Yet I adhere to it – as I meant it; i.e., that the best and most typical English diarists would probably have been bores if they had not kept diaries – for they possessed that first attribute of the bore, the need to mention everything. And now, after much reading of diaries, and while allowing for all kinds of exceptions, the feeling I am left with is that the traditional, the generic English diary, from Pepys and Evelyn through the parsons and the political gossips to Crabb Robinson and Queen Victoria, is the escape, the safety-valve of the otherwise bore, the bright reverse of natural dullness. Facts, actions, lists of things and people, details of movement, exact information, plain observation – all valuable and some enchanting, as it happens, after fifty or a hundred years – but *accidentally* so; not designed expression, not making the exciting claims of works of art, but set down in routine, because of somebody's neat habit. Lucky for us. How much luckier we are, after all, to know Crabb Robinson in his diaries, as a whole, with all his illustrious friends massed about him on parade, than to have been mere acquaintances in his time of the busy, ubiquitous, unremarkable man with the absurdly crowded engagement-book!

The women diarists are in a special case however. They are not as a genus bores *manquées*, because they very likely would not have been diarists if they could have been something more directly self-expressive. They are diarists *faute de mieux*, whether they knew it or not. Dorothy Wordsworth kept journals and did no more creative writing only because, consciously or unconsciously, she had decided that devotion to William was her clearest and most necessary duty; Fanny Burney wrote diaries because she should have been training herself to be a great novelist and had not enough decisiveness for that, so escaped, with ease and brilliance; Miss Weeton wrote them because she was obscure and lost, half-mad with a sense of frustration, and the need to say something, somehow; Caroline Fox was a natural intellectual who played second fiddle modestly to all her brilliant male friends. And the Queen? The Queen is above common rules, and in any case Victoria sweeps them away, as she should, by being perhaps at once a diarist *and* a bore.

to it owing to some anonymous letter from the usual boy Jones, w
ned to come across d in one anoth
rawing attention to g up to a dome
s and the erring er lord and ma
her knees and pr tears in her
possibly with me time as q
y there were othe ical bias, believ
dn't make the t man, or men
ral, were always about a lady, e
ing she was the b of argument, wh
ose to be tired o ions on her w
er intent, the up ed on another,
of many *liaisons* b nen getting on
d forty and young s cases of femin
tion proved up to

was a thousand pi llowance of brai
neighbour obviously was, should waste his valuable time with proflig
f who might present him with a nice dose to last him his lifetime.
ure of single blessedness he would one day take unto himself a wife wh
Miss Right came on the scene but in the interim ladies' society wa
sine qua non though he had the gravest possible doubts, not that
in the smallest to pump Stephen about Miss Ferguson as to whet
uld find much satisfaction basking in the boy and girl courts
d the company of smirking misses without a penny to their nar
tri-weekly with the orthodox preliminary canter of complimentpay
lking out leading up to fond lovers' ways and flowers and chocs.
f him house and homeless, rooked by some landlady worse than
ther, was really too bad at his age. The queer suddenly things

Afterword

ANTHONY BURGESS

THE Nazis and Japanese were beaten, and Britain rather reluctantly emerged from her brave isolation. She also ceased to be the ruler of a great empire: the peoples of the East saw that white giants could be, if only temporarily, trounced by yellow dwarfs, and that the appearance of a majestic order had been fraudulently sustained by a few functionaries with bare knees. But England had bequeathed to her former colonies an inestimable gift – the English language – and it is proper to speak of the post-war literature of that language as being apportioned between the British Commonwealth and the United States of America: England herself became a mere province in literature as in the domain of world politics.

Elizabeth Bowen had seen the contemporary glory of the novel best manifested in E. M. Forster and Virginia Woolf – two figures who were later diminished as 'Bloomsbury', though Virginia Woolf was to gain a new glory as the matron saint of women's liberation. The first considerable fiction of post-war England was to be international in style and subject; it was to render visions unthinkable in the blander tradition which Elizabethan Bowen had celebrated. With *Animal Farm* and *Nineteen Eighty-Four*, George Orwell wrote more like a European than an Englishman, and he showed that the totalitarian nightmare Britain had watched others live through represented a pattern for the future, not the past: the days of Forsterian liberalism were over. There was another nightmare too, fruit of Hiroshima and Nagasaki. Aldous Huxley, living in California but still an Englishman, prophesied post-atomic barbarism in *Ape and Essence*, and L. P. Hartley, who had been considered a milder and smaller Henry James, produced a haunting image of collective nuclear guilt in *Facial Justice*.

Great war fiction could be reasonably expected from a nation which had endured Nazi aggression longer than any other, but Britain produced nothing which could be compared with what came out of America.

Anthony Burgess, photographed in the 1970s.

Norman Mailer's *The Naked and the Dead* remains the best fictional record of the war in the Pacific, while James Jones's *From Here to Eternity* and Herman Wouk's *The Caine Mutiny*, though less 'literary', are crammed with hard factual material about what it was like to fight in the US Army and Navy respectively. With Wouk's later gigantic novels *The Winds of War* and *War and Remembrance*, the task of recording the entire world conflict in fictional form was effected in a somewhat contrived but generally convincing fashion. Out of Britain came Evelyn Waugh's *Sword of Honour*, a trilogy which restricts the experience of the war to a patrician Catholic infantry officer, makes comedy of horror, and is more concerned with those changes in society of which war is both a symptom and a catalyst, than with the fighting experience in itself. *Sword of Honour* could be taken as an updated version of Ford Madox Ford's great war tetralogy *Parade's End* (unnoticed by Elizabeth Bowen) – a work much re-read or newly discovered in the late 'forties and 'fifties. It was as though, lacking a sizeable novel about the conflict we had just suffered, we were forced to go back to the war of our fathers.

Elizabeth Bowen herself presented, very brilliantly, the atmosphere of what used to be called the 'home front' in *The Heat of the Day*, as Graham Greene conveyed the feeling of wartime West Africa in *The Heart of the Matter* and the shattering of windows and dustiness of air-raid shelters in *The End of the Affair*. In both authors the war is a somewhat marginal matter, a mere décor. It was left to Olivia Manning to present, with remarkable insight, the experiences of a British soldier in the Western desert in the *Levant Trilogy* which completed the wartime chronicle of Harriet and Guy Pringle in her previous *Balkan Trilogy*. But, I repeat, Britain produced nothing to compare with American war fiction, and no serving soldier seemed to have either the heart or the literary talent to convert his experiences into fiction which transcended the comic, the facetious, the tendentious, or (as with popular sub-Conradian novels like Nicholas Monsarrat's *The Cruel Sea*) the merely thrilling.

Not that English novelists lacked either skill to engage the large canvas or the expressive equipment to deal with large themes – so long as the theme was not the recent war faced head on. C. P. Snow wrote a *roman fleuve* entitled *Strangers and Brothers* which examined the locations of power in a new meritocratic England, and Anthony Powell, in *A Dance to the Music of Time*, tried Proustianly to memorialize the region in British society where the bohemian and the patrician meet. But in the pentateuch called *Children of Violence* Doris Lessing brought to fiction in English

(left) *Aldous Huxley, photographed by Cecil Beaton. In 1937 Huxley settled permanently in California and there experimented with mysticism and narcotics as mental release from a reality that he found increasingly repulsive.*

(below left) *Doris Lessing: her novels, which range in genre from autobiography to science fiction, treat political and social subjects – especially the position of women – with psychological intensity and great documentary detail.*

(below right) *Evelyn Waugh as a young man, painted by Henry Lamb. After the Second World War the brilliant satire of his early works gave way to a more pronounced handling of religious themes.*

themes very different from those of the bluff Snow and the polished Powell. These themes – racial and sexual struggle – were to dominate her work and fuse at last in a kind of apocalyptical vision of the agony of the dispossessed. A narrower view than hers would have found something wrong merely in capitalism, or the patriarchal tradition of western society, or colonial exploitation, but, with the help of R. D. Laing, she has questioned our received notions of human sanity. The novel as surveyed by Elizabeth Bowen had no doubts about the nature of sanity, as it had no doubts about society, or ethics, or the relationship between the sexes. The new fiction in English was beginning to ask questions previously considered indecent, or anarchic, or improper for mere literary diversion.

Doris Lessing was brought up in Rhodesia, and she was not the only African, white or black, to help bring a new urgency to the novel. There was Nadine Gordimer from the Cape, as there were Chinua Achebe and Cyprian Ekwensis from Nigeria. The last word on India had been considered to have been uttered by Forster, but the Indians themselves were now creating images of India from the inside – R. K. Narayan, Raja Rao – and the Caribbean, with V. S. Naipaul, Samuel Selvon, Edgar Mittelholzer, and British Guiana, with Wilson Harris, were giving voice. Even novelists born in Britain seemed dissatisfied with what looked like an increasingly limited subject-matter in the post-war Welfare State. Paul Scott did what Kipling ought to have done (though, alas, with less genius) – served up the whole panorama of India in his *Raj Quartet*. I myself had to go to Malaya to learn how to write fiction. Lawrence Durrell was poetically, sometimes hysterically, inspired by Alexandria. And, at the same time, those once disregarded transplantations of English society in the antipodes were speaking up. New Zealand produced Janet Frame and Maurice Shadbolt, and Australia recorded its first Nobel prizeman in Patrick White.

White may now, if he wishes, declare himself a homosexual, like Sir Angus Wilson. There was no true homosexual literature before the war. Forster, whose deplorable though honestly homosexual novel *Maurice* appeared posthumously, had had to keep quiet about his endowment. Works like *Hemlock and After* tell very candidly of the social penumbra where pederasty operates, though, typically, it had to be left to America, with Gore Vidal's *The City and the Pillar*, to bring homosexuality first into the open. Radclyffe Hall, with her ill-written *The Well of Loneliness*, had suffered suppression in 1929, but lesbian novels were now free to be published, as were heterosexual ones which presented frankly the erotic

Kingsley Amis, poet and novelist: his first novel was Lucky Jim, *a comic account of a teacher at a provincial university; his succeeding novels have been equally funny and increasingly scornful.*

experience from the woman's point of view. Not even the male ecstasy had been permitted total candour of expression in the period Elizabeth Bowen summarizes, but, in the 'sixties, there were no further restrictions. As Philip Larkin puts it,

> Sexual intercourse began
> In 1963 . . .
> Between the end of the Chatterley ban
> And the Beatles' first LP.

The Beatles may have no place in a brief survey of literature, but they represented a movement, or perhaps the ultimate popularization of a movement, which began ten years earlier than sexual intercourse. With the publication of Kingsley Amis's *Lucky Jim*, with which we can associate John Wain's *Hurry On Down*, John Braine's *Room at the Top* and Alan

Sillitoe's *Saturday Night and Sunday Morning*, the ruled, as opposed to the ruling, irrupted into literature. These books do not stand for a true literature of revolt – they are hardly at all political – but they claim for the sons of the workers, especially in the provinces, a right to speak which, in the Elizabeth Bowen time, had been monopolized by the nation's capital, the older universities and the upper middle class. While the hero of Wain's novel does what Orwell invited all the middle class to do – to drop their aitches if they could but certainly to identify themselves with the proletariat – the other heroes (or anti-heroes, as they began to be called) demand no more than a minimal material justice from society – enough money for beer and fags and the chance to date a high-class woman. Braine's Joe Lampton actually marries one: this is known as hypergamy.

With Amis, an Oxonian and a university lecturer, there was a plea for greater honesty among so-called intellectuals (a term which has always been embarrassing in England, though not in France) – a willingness to say that Henry James is a bore when he is a bore, and not to cold-shoulder such sub-literature as the James Bond spy story and the whole genre of science fiction. Artistic honesty was a feature of post-war Britain, along with an attempt to remove the barrier between demotic and aristocratic diversion. Freddie Ayer, the philosopher, could declare himself a football fan; Philip Larkin could admit that he had been inspired to write poetry by popular song lyrics of the 'thirties and, when not being a poet and librarian in Hull, reviewed jazz records; the most highbrow claimed to adore the Beatles. Science fiction, which had been a toy of H. G. Wells, became a literary specialization with specialist reviewers.

The trouble generally with the English novel was the lack of anything to write about. There were countless novels, many loudly acclaimed, some the winners of prizes, which dealt with adultery on Primrose Hill, and they were usually by women. Britain was out of things, but everyone was protected by the Welfare State. High taxation and holidays in Spain seemed insufficient material for serious fiction. Nevertheless, by dint of acceptance of foreign ideas, such as existentialism and structuralism, the British novel managed to survive. Iris Murdoch wrote an existentialist novel in *Under the Net* and a structuralist one in *A Severed Head*, and it was discovered that Ivy Compton-Burnett (unnoticed by Elizabeth Bowen) had been writing structuralist fiction for decades. John Fowles experimented and made money; B. S. Johnson experimented and cut his wrists in the bath. Christine Brooke-Rose followed the *anti-romanciers*. Other novelists, like William Golding, found absolute evil a suitable fictional property. But, in general, the British novel (meaning the novel of the Commonwealth) was recognized as 'less significant' than the novels of American Jews like Saul Bellow and Philip Roth, of American Southerners like William Styron and, an acknowledged giant, William Faulkner, and of American blacks like Ralph Ellison and James Baldwin. America was where the action was, and also the money. A British novelist could receive a million dollars advance if he restricted himself to espionage. But the world knew that the cream, fresh or sour, of twentieth-century experience was to be consumed only in America, and in Britain you tasted only weak tea and wrapped bread.

The British did better in the drama. Because the British produced Shakespeare, it does not follow that they have a special claim on the genre. The later pages of Graham Greene's survey record a dismal West End record. Before the war began, some had hailed the verse drama of Eliot and of Auden and Isherwood as opening new doors, or curtains, and the post-war period saw in both Eliot's *The Cocktail Party* and Christopher Fry's *The Lady's Not For Burning* evidence of a recovered vitality in a form which, since it had survived the war, might set a pattern for the peace. Because of cricketing associations, Eliot and Fry appeared in the same critical headlines, but it was cruel to compare Eliot's seriousness of craft and purpose with the plastic facetiousness of Fry. After these two there were no further takers in the medium, except in drama festivals at the English cathedrals, and it was seen that, after all, the future of the drama might well lie in colloquial prose.

From 1948 until 1954 I was, as a college teacher of drama, concerned with the production of plays above the *George and Margaret* and *Quiet Week End* level, and there was not much that was both new and worthy, at least not in Britain. Arthur Miller was good, but American accents are always difficult for British actors. Terence Rattigan, entertaining, well made, continued the pre-war West End tradition. It was not until 1956 that anyone could speak with conviction of a future for the English theatre. This was the year of John Osborne's *Look Back in Anger*, a play which, from one aspect, can be characterized as an orthodox three-acter with a fixed set, but, from another, must be seen as a blazing indictment of British hypocrisy, class prejudice, imaginative debility, sanctimonious-ness, and all the national vices which, even during a desperate war, had been paraded as virtues.

Jimmy Porter, the anti-hero, was the prototypical 'angry young man', the provincial redbrick beneficiary of state education who had achieved

John Osborne's Look Back in Anger *at the Royal Court Theatre in 1957. Left to right: Kenneth Haigh as Jimmy Porter, Alan Bates as Cliff Lewis and Mary Ure as Alison Porter. Set in an attic flat in the Midlands, the play centres on Jimmy Porter, the archetypal 'angry young man' – embittered, rebellious and disillusioned with life in post-war Britain.*

hypergamy but was still not satisfied. His voice was that of the too long dispossessed, but, like D. H. Lawrence, he spoke not just for a social class but for the whole of an England which had been a raging lion but was now a toy lamb. The establishment of egalitarianism in Britain had solved no real problems, nor had the dismantling of an empire. Nobody starved, but the life had gone out of the nation.

Osborne's anger became a blowpipe flame capable of being turned in a variety of directions. In *Luther*, the great reformer is angry at Tetzel's sale of indulgences. Angry words are not enough; angry farts are necessary too. Visceral eloquence rather than a Shavian consistency of philosophy was Osborne's contribution to the theatre. There was no more room for tepid gentility: the kitchen sink was on the stage, not french windows leading to a tennis court. The provinces and the articulate working-class replaced the bourgeoisie of Lonsdale, Galsworthy, Maugham and Coward. Coarse words and actions made Rattigan's 'Aunt Edna' tut.

Theatre does not need philosophy; it needs vigorous dialectic. But a view of life is the engine of a dialectic, and there was a recognizable view of life, or congeries of cognate views, behind the new plays – whether of Harold Pinter, N. F. Simpson, Edward Bond or John Arden. Camus and Sartre in France taught a new tragic destiny for man. Man was an absurdity in the face of the wheeling galaxies; he was committed to action, which was the only way to define his humanity, but action led him nowhere. In Beckett's *Waiting for Godot*, which had first been put on in Paris a few years before the Osborne eruption in London, a pair of the totally dispossessed wait for a revelation which they know will not come, and they endlessly talk without communicating anything. In Ionesco's absurdist plays even less is communicated; the syntax of action as well as speech is broken, and discontinuity of events symbolizes our discovery of a lack of meaning in the universe. While playwrights like Osborne and Arnold Wesker stuck to social themes, Pinter exploited the problems of verbal communication. He also, and this is probably his main achievement, showed that there are unspoken meanings underlying and contradicting speech, and that these can articulate themselves only in violence. The new drama was capable of more violence than the Agatha Christie gunshot. In Edward Bond's *Saved* a group of louts batter to death a baby in a pram. The violence is not gratuitous; it is the incarnation of a philosophy.

It is always futile to try to summarize drama in terms of its content. Tom Stoppard, who has brought to the stage not only the problems of Central European politics (he is of Czech origin) but also metaphysics and epistemology, said once that he could happily listen to stage dialectic without expecting it to reach a conclusion. And the strength of the new British theatre lies in the vigour of its rhetoric, not what that rhetoric is about. Rhetoric does not mean the contrivance of impressive tropes or, as a term of disparagement, the invocation of outdated verbal glories (as in Stephen Phillips or Christopher Fry): it is essentially the language of conviction, and yet the conviction need have no validity outside the terms of art. Here the drama differs from the novel.

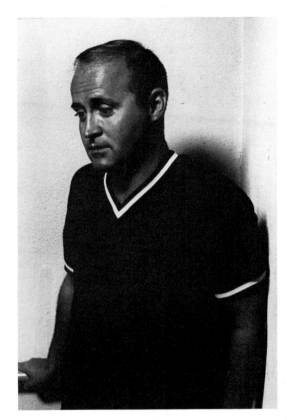

(above left) *Samuel Beckett, drawn by Avigdor Arikha in 1971. Beckett has spent most of his life in Paris and many of his works have been written first in French.*

(above right) *Edward Bond in 1965, the year in which* Saved *shocked audiences in London. The banning of* Early Morning *(1968), a satire about Queen Victoria, led to the abolition of stage censorship in England.*

(right) *Tom Stoppard, photographed by his wife Miriam. His plays are comedies written by a philosopher: sparkling verbal ingenuity in part conceals deeply felt ethical concerns.*

(left) *Harold Pinter on the set of* A Kind of Alaska, *one of a trilogy of plays* Other Places, *first performed at the National Theatre in London in 1982. The actress in the bed is Judi Dench. Pinter established his reputation with plays whose characters' motivations often remain mysterious but whose speech mirrors everyday fragmentary conversation and silences with a realistic elusiveness of mood.*

T. S. Eliot, by Cecil Beaton. The summit of Eliot's poetic career was the publication of Four Quartets *(1943), profound meditations on Christian experience. After the war he experimented with verse drama.*

Graham Greene, at the conclusion of his essay, grants the future of the theatre two possibilities: 'Now we are heading either for chaos of such long duration that the theatre will not survive our civilization, or a world so new and changed it may well be that in the theatre it will seem as though Elizabeth were on the throne again.' Nay, I know not seem. The deutero-Elizabethan drama may not be as great as the proto, but it is valid for our time, and we ask no more. Like Greene, I had the opportunity to see the BBC's first television in the 1930s and the historic production of Pirandello's *The Man With A Flower In His Mouth*. Here, as it transpired, was a new art of drama, and a very considerable one. Most of us see most of our plays on the small screen, a difficult and searching medium, and have noted that it is as capable of framing greatness as the West End proscenium arch. To say that it is not 'literature' is to admit the same of the older art. Drama can, as with Shakespeare, be literature if it wishes, but its primary obligation is not literary at all.

Poetry is literature in excelsis, the exploitation to the limit of the possibilities of language, and its post-war direction was, perhaps, visible, in the perspective of the 1940s. Eliot had completed the first of his *Four Quartets* in 1935, Dylan Thomas had published acclaimed verse just before the war, and Auden was established as a major poet. Long before, indeed, Eliot's *Prufrock* and Pound's *Sextus Propertius* had made the year 1917 the year 1 of modern poetry, but perhaps the two poets, not being English, were not really producing in England.

The question 'What is English poetry?' is one that Cecil, granted his patriotic commission, could not easily answer. For, with Eliot, an American, in England and Auden, an Englishman, in America, it was already evident that national boundaries had ceased to mean very much. It may fancifully be said that the labour of wresting significance out of words and rhythms is so great that matters of landscape and accent become unimportant: let great poetry in English come where it will, and let us be thankful for it.

The Second World War, then, ended as it began, with Eliot, Auden and Dylan Thomas pre-eminent. As with the other war, serving soldiers, sailors and airmen produced little, except for poets like Roy Fuller and Henry Reed, and the 'war poet' did not properly exist. As Cecil Day Lewis had said,

> It is the logic of our times,
> No subject for immortal verse,
> That we, who lived on honest dreams,
> Defend the bad against the worse.

Four Quartets was only marginally about the war, and Dylan Thomas's followers of the 'New Apocalypse' dealt in images which could be about anything and probably were. As for the verse of Auden, which increasingly had a Christian content (Thomas's merely had a Biblical one), it located good and evil elsewhere than on battlefields. The old political preoccupations had gone, and they went too with Day Lewis and Stephen Spender. Spender had become more a delegate at international conferences that a practising poet, and Day Lewis turned from communism to Thomas Hardy, preparing himself for the laureateship.

If the major poets generally stayed out of the war, one major poet was very much involved in it, and on the wrong side. This, of course, was Ezra Pound, who brayed antisemitism and curses on the Allies from Rome radio, was declared a traitor and then mad, and yet in the *Pisan Cantos* produced perhaps the finest verse of the period. His case raised a central problem of art: how far can good art be created by bad men? There is a cognate question: how far can good art be appreciated by bad men? This can be answered: all the way. The Nazis loved Beethoven and Brahms, if not Mendelssohn, which argues that at least one art is beyond morality. Might not this be true of all the arts? Questions as to whether Eliot was antisemitic began to be raised ('The jew is underneath the lot'), and Yeats's antipopulism (the poor at the nobleman's gate) was considered to harm his poetry, but the wise saw the uncovenanted power of art and found that few poets' statements could be taken at their face value.

As Dylan Thomas never made plain statements, except when needing money or another drink, he was always safe, but, looking back from the 'eighties, we see now that that could not after all be said of his craft or sullen art. He has certainly not survived as an influence, and the main stream of Anglo-American poetry settled early on to statements uncoloured by surrealism or apocalypse. On both sides of the Atlantic poets generally found the seventeenth century a golden age, with 'metaphysical' wit congenial and a more or less strict stanza preferable to free verse. This was the tradition that Americans like Wallace Stevens, John Crowe Ransom and Allen Tate followed, and William Empson's *Seven Types of Ambiguity* (published in 1930 but ignored by Cecil) justified complexities and even contradictions which only solidity of structure could reconcile.

So in Robert Lowell and John Berryman we find traditional forms like the sonnet, and we find the poets freed from the burden of an original philosophy by their acceptance of the Catholic faith. In England there was an empiricism which forbade overmuch intrusion of the intellect and a willingness to make verse out of the quotidian and even trivial, so long as the verse could be made well. Philip Larkin writes about what happens to a Hull librarian who falls in love or sees death approaching in the shape of a postman, and both he and Kingsley Amis can approach, without loss of formal rigour, the stances of 'light verse'. With Sir John Betjeman, poet laureate, everything looks like light verse, and the prosodic struggles of Hopkins and Clough and Whitman were suffered in vain. No English poet – Peter Redgrove, Martin Bell, Peter Porter – has been trivial as, say,

Charles Tennyson Turner and T. E. Brown were trivial, but some of them have seemed lightweight in comparison with non-English poets whose gravity of utterance concealed technique less sure-footed than that of their fellows in Britain. Alan Ginsberg, for instance, whose *Howl* is often ridiculous (the best minds of his generation driven to madness indeed) but is excused by its ambition and its willingness to resurrect the long irregular line of Whitman in the service of grandiloquence. This is the verse of 'protest', though what, except everything, the poet is protesting against is not clear. English poetry remained a poetry of acceptance, of a minimally qualified yes, and this makes it a kind of piano music with the soft pedal down.

It is the Celts who have brought to poetry in English qualities un-suburban and serious. Since Yeats, Pound and Eliot the English have been asking themselves uneasily whether, after all, the indigenous genius which bred Keats, Browning and Hopkins may not have departed the land. At the moment, it is Seamus Heaney who is emerging as the major cisatlantic voice in English, and the power of his work may owe something to the fact that he has a subject-matter, whereas the English have not. So long as Ireland suffers, Irish poets can sing. Scotland, too, underwent a factitious kind of suffering in the art of Hugh MacDiarmid, who was conceivably the greatest poet, in any language, of the entire century. MacDiarmid wrote in the English which was his mother tongue when he was the young Christopher Grieve, and also in a Lallans painfully and artificially learnt. His philosophy was as wrong as Pound's though it was Stalin and not Mussolini who was his patron saint, but a philosophy can be merely a starting-point for a poet. MacDiarmid's greatness lies in a technique which can absorb anything and in an idiolect capable of ranging from the austerest intellectuality to the most direct physical experience. Even when transcribing prose into verse he seems to sing.

If I have said (though little enough) more about the novel than drama and poetry, and if I say nothing at all about the keepers of diaries and journals, this is not just because the novel is the literary form I myself practise and the journal is the mere raw material for the rest of literature, but more especially the novel. It seems to me that the novel is established as the major literary form of the age and that, as Joyce showed in *Ulysses*, it is capable of absorbing the other forms. The drama has, after the expansive efforts of Wagner and his disciple Shaw, accepted limitations imposed by commerce; since *The Waste Land* and the unfinished *Cantos*, only Ted Hughes's *Crow* stands as a successful example of the long poem. The novel can still be what Lawrence called the bright book of life, and its powers of synthesis have hardly yet been seen.

If another war came, using limited armaments and isolating England behind its battlements once more, would it be possible to commemorate English literature again in the manner of this little book? The historical subject-matter – up to the point where the authors turn shy – would be the same, but I think the approach might be different. There would be more emphasis on England's debt to Europe, a hint of regret that British writers were less concerned with formal perfection than their European counterparts, and perhaps even a willingness – learnt from Eliot – to concede that our literature lost as much as it gained when the Protestant reformation and the Puritan revolution severed it from the cultures of Italy and France. More than anything, English literature would seem not quite so much a preserve of the ruling class, and the implied aesthetic would be at once more exacting and less genteel. For we ourselves modify the past, and we are not quite the people we were when government posters proclaimed: 'Your courage, your steadfastness, your patience' (or whatever the prescribed virtues were) 'will bring us victory.'

A detail from the title-page of Ezra Pound's Pisan Cantos *(1948), perhaps his masterpiece. The drawing of the poet is by his friend the Vorticist artist Henri Gaudier-Brzeska.*

SOURCES OF ILLUSTRATIONS

INDEX

Page numbers in *italics* refer to illustrations